everyday
DIVINE

†

A Catholic Guide
to Active Spirituality

MARY DeTURRIS POUST

ALPHA

A member of Penguin Group (USA) Inc.

ALPHA BOOKS

Published by Penguin Group (USA) Inc.

Penguin Group (USA) Inc., 375 Hudson Street, New York, New York 10014, USA • Penguin Group (Canada), 90 Eglinton Avenue East, Suite 700, Toronto, Ontario M4P 2Y3, Canada (a division of Pearson Penguin Canada Inc.) • Penguin Books Ltd., 80 Strand, London WC2R 0RL, England • Penguin Ireland, 25 St. Stephen's Green, Dublin 2, Ireland (a division of Penguin Books Ltd.) • Penguin Group (Australia), 250 Camberwell Road, Camberwell, Victoria 3124, Australia (a division of Pearson Australia Group Pty. Ltd.) • Penguin Books India Pvt. Ltd., 11 Community Centre, Panchsheel Park, New Delhi—110 017, India • Penguin Group (NZ), 67 Apollo Drive, Rosedale, North Shore, Auckland 1311, New Zealand (a division of Pearson New Zealand Ltd.) • Penguin Books (South Africa) (Pty.) Ltd., 24 Sturdee Avenue, Rosebank, Johannesburg 2196, South Africa • Penguin Books Ltd., Registered Offices: 80 Strand, London WC2R 0RL, England

Copyright © 2012 by Mary DeTurris Poust

International Standard Book Number: 978-1-61564-200-7
Library of Congress Catalog Card Number: 2012939809

14   13   12   8   7   6   5   4   3   2   1

Interpretation of the printing code: The rightmost number of the first series of numbers is the year of the book's printing; the rightmost number of the second series of numbers is the number of the book's printing. For example, a printing code of 12-1 shows that the first printing occurred in 2012.

Printed in the United States of America

Note: This publication contains the opinions and ideas of its author. It is intended to provide helpful and informative material on the subject matter covered. It is sold with the understanding that the author and publisher are not engaged in rendering professional services in the book. If the reader requires personal assistance or advice, a competent professional should be consulted.

The author and publisher specifically disclaim any responsibility for any liability, loss, or risk, personal or otherwise, which is incurred as a consequence, directly or indirectly, of the use and application of any of the contents of this book.

Trademarks: All terms mentioned in this book that are known to be or are suspected of being trademarks or service marks have been appropriately capitalized. Alpha Books and Penguin Group (USA) Inc. cannot attest to the accuracy of this information. Use of a term in this book should not be regarded as affecting the validity of any trademark or service mark.

Most Alpha books are available at special quantity discounts for bulk purchases for sales promotions, premiums, fund-raising, or educational use. Special books, or book excerpts, can also be created to fit specific needs. For details, write: Special Markets, Alpha Books, 375 Hudson Street, New York, NY 10014.

ALWAYS LEARNING   PEARSON

For Dennis,
my best friend,
my partner in all things,
my soul mate, my love

CONTENTS

Appendixes

INTRODUCTION

Developing a regular and ever-deepening prayer life sounds fantastic on the surface, but it can be a tough thing to put into practice. Life gets in the way. *We* get in the way. We may want to pray with all our heart, but when it comes down to it, there just aren't enough hours in the day. How do we fit prayer into our already busy schedules, and what's the right way to pray anyway?

I wrote this book to answer those questions, not only for my readers but for myself. As a lifelong Catholic, prayer has always been part of my life, and yet I was finding it increasingly difficult to stick with a routine, to pray amid the chaos and insanity of my life as a wife, mother of three, and full-time writer who works out of a basement office surrounded by Barbie dolls, a video game console, and a towering cat condo. I had to find a way to make prayer part of my everyday actions, or I risked losing my spiritual foothold completely.

So I began exploring everyday prayer practices, starting with a spiritual breakfast routine and expanding to prayer while driving, prayer while waiting, and prayer while cleaning. And guess what? It works. I think I realized it in a big way on my first-ever silent retreat a few years ago. I went out for a walk through the woods and found myself rushing down the trail like I was racing to catch the E train in New York City during rush hour. But in this case, I had nowhere to go and all day to get there.

So I stopped, took a deep breath, and started to look and listen to the world around me. Next thing I knew, I saw little flashes of orange in the leaves ahead of me. I stopped again. Tiny efts—which are baby newts according to my son—were darting across my path. They would have been under my feet had I continued at my previous pace. I would have missed them completely, these amazing little pieces of God's great creation. I started thinking about all the other things I must be missing as I run through life, my mind always somewhere else. How could I slow down my thinking, my movement, and start to see the sacred in my own life?

Enter everyday prayer. By weaving prayer into the actions of daily life—showering, cooking, cleaning, driving, working, eating, jogging, and more—you can bring a sense of the divine to everything you do. Suddenly life isn't the chore you might imagine it to be; it's a joy, because everyday prayer makes you grateful, shows you where God enters into your busy life, helps you traverse the highs and lows with equal calmness.

I hope, as you work your way through this book, you, too, will discover the sacredness of your own life, the places where faith intersects with the everyday, where God has always been present.

So much of what you'll read comes right out of the pages of my own prayer life and the lives of others who were willing to share their stories, their practices, their struggles, and their successes. Learn from them, but don't be afraid to spread your wings and create your own methods and practices.

Whether you're a veteran pray-er or building a spiritual practice from the ground up, the journey ahead is a magnificent one. Savor it, sink into it, let your entire being be infused by prayer in one form or another, and watch where it takes you.

EVERYDAY EXTRAS

Throughout this book, you'll find special messages and other extra information to help you better understand certain aspects of everyday prayer and to help you see the practical applications of this kind of spirituality. Here's what to watch for:

Practical Wisdom

These sidebars include quotes and observations on prayer life from famous saints throughout history, popes, contemporary Catholic writers, and more.

Moving Meditation

Put what you read into practice through these brief exercises that provide you with specific ways to bring prayer into your everyday life.

Notes from the Journey

Sometimes the best way to take the next step on the prayer path is to hear directly from someone who's been there. These journal entries are real experiences taken from my own spiritual life—the joys, the struggles, the questions—in hopes that they'll help you in yours.

EXERCISES AND RESOURCES

In the appendixes at the back of the book, you'll find a compendium of vital information for going forward after you're done reading. The book itself can be used in daily prayer, but if you want to look up a specific prayer or practical application quickly, check the back. There you'll find a collection of classic Catholic prayers; a series of 10 everyday prayer exercises to help jump-start your spiritual life; and a resource section with suggested reading, helpful websites, and even prayer apps for your smartphone. It's all about working the divine into everything, every day.

ACKNOWLEDGMENTS

I have to start my acknowledgments for this book by going to the source and thanking God for the gift of faith. It's a gift I didn't earn, a gift I didn't deserve, but there it is nonetheless. It has come to me in the form of faithful people who have taught me by their example, from the earliest days of my childhood up to the present day. Never doubt the power of one person, one action to make a difference in the faith life of another. This gift of faith is mysterious and awesome and totally what I should expect from a God as loving and powerful as ours, and yet I'm always surprised.

After God, there's no one more deserving of my thanks than my family—my husband, Dennis, and our three children, Noah, Olivia, and Chiara—who are my daily connection to the divine. Our domestic church may be noisy, but it's filled with faith and love just the same. Thank you, thank you, thank you for putting up with me as I wrote this book and reached previously unforeseen levels of stress. You are all amazing, and I am eternally grateful for your love and support.

A special thank you to all those people who offered to share their prayer practices with me, by phone, by email, and in person. I am so grateful for your kindness and generosity, especially when I'd tell you I needed your answers in less than 24 hours. I am humbled by your example of faith and your commitment to prayer in its many different forms.

I would also like to thank my agent, Marilyn Allen, and everyone at Alpha, including Lori Cates Hand, Christy Wagner, and Kayla Dugger.

Finally, I would like to thank you, my fellow traveler on the spiritual journey. We are pilgrims, searching for God in the here and now, walking a common path toward heaven, gathering strength from each other as we go. Thank you for taking the next step on this journey with me through the pages of this book.

1

CREATING CALM AMID THE CHAOS

Modern life moves at breakneck speed, and if you're like most, you probably get caught up in the whirlwind despite your best attempts to keep things on an even keel. You run from one obligation to the next, longing for a space apart, a still point where you can remain centered even as life ebbs and flows around you.

In the recesses of your heart, you may imagine a retreat, a vacation, even just one hour of quiet time where you can hear yourself think and maybe hear the Spirit whispering to your soul. But solitude, silence, and spiritual respite are seen as luxuries in our culture, bonus prizes you can claim only after you've done everything else on your endless to-do list.

So you put prayer and serenity into the "someday" category, thinking you'll get around to it when the kids are older, when the house repairs are finished, when you retire, when you get through your busy season .... But the busy seasons never seem to end, and *someday* never arrives.

It doesn't have to be that way. In fact, it *shouldn't* be that way, at least not if you want to lead a happy, healthy life that fills you with inner peace and satisfaction rather than dread and discontent. When you begin to see prayer not as something that happens outside your everyday actions but as the thread that weaves together the disparate parts of your life tapestry, you soon discover a connection to the divine that never dissipates, never wavers, even when the world outside is pounding on the door to your soul demanding to be let in.

You *can* have it all, despite the seemingly obvious contradictions—a still point while in constant motion, silence in the midst of never-ending noise, sacred vibrations running through the most mundane moments.

DESPERATELY SEEKING SERENITY

Every night before I close my eyes, I think about the morning and imagine how peaceful my day is going to be. I'll get up and say Morning Prayer. I'll greet my three children and their many demands of the day with a quiet smile, content in my vocation as a mother. I'll give my husband a kiss good-bye as he heads off to work and then spend the first 20 minutes of my workday in silent meditation.

That plan usually goes out the window by the second time I hit the snooze button.

The teenager has overslept and has to be driven to school. The tween needs someone to help her study for her social studies test, and the 6-year-old is worried that I'll forget to save the almost-empty milk jug she needs for her class project. Before I know it, I am silently—and sometimes not so silently—screaming, "Serenity now!" à la *Seinfeld*'s Frank Costanza.

Bringing the peace of prayer into your busy life isn't as easy as just wishing it will be so, or even *saying* it will be so. When it comes to prayer, all talk and no action leads nowhere fast, and before you know it, you're throwing up your hands in frustration and figuring you'll try again tomorrow, next week, someday, ...

I have been comforted by the knowledge that I'm not alone in the constant quest for spiritual calm in my mostly chaotic life. I talk about it with friends, hear about it from strangers in the comment section of my blog, and absorb it on a large scale in retreat settings where everyone—no matter what their background, no matter what their faith—seems to be hungry for the exact same thing: inner peace.

Deep down, I know prayer is the one thing that can redirect the negatives and transform my actions and my life once and for all. And yet I resist. Why is it so hard to pray?

It comes down to the way most of us view prayer. We think we need hours of downtime, so prayer becomes an improbability, maybe even an impossibility. We think we need to be in a church, or at the very least on our knees, and how often can we do that? The answer lies not in finding more hours in the day but in changing our perspective.

Practical Wisdom

Prayer is not simply some necessary compartment in the daily schedule of a Christian or a source of support in time of need, nor is it restricted to Sunday mornings or mealtimes. Praying is living. It is eating and drinking, action and rest, teaching and learning, playing and working. Praying pervades every aspect of our lives.

—Henri Nouwen, "With Open Hands," *The Only Necessary Thing*

WHEN DID LIFE GET SO COMPLICATED?

Think about the way everyday life has changed in recent decades, especially in the past few years. Do you remember the days when you used to be able to take the phone off the hook if you didn't want to talk to someone, or just let it ring and ring and ring? No call waiting, no answering machines, no texting. Now you're connected 24/7. Whether you're at work, on the road, eating dinner, or on vacation, you're probably in constant communication with the office, family, friends, the school district, soccer club, advertisers, and random folks who track you down and send you things you don't want. The new normal is not built for prayerfulness, silence, or, for that matter, sanity.

Of course, you could turn the tables and consider how difficult life used to be not all that long ago, before you had a microwave and email, a cell phone and online shopping. It's not all bad; it's just different.

Fortunately, prayer is adaptable. You can bend it and stretch it and mold it to fit even the craziest life configurations. You can use ancient, low-tech methods of prayer to navigate your modern, high-speed world.

"I Don't Have Time to Pray"

I can imagine what you're thinking right about now. You want to pray; you *need* to pray. But sitting down to pray while the rest of the world is running around like mad seems, well, irresponsible. Guess what? No one said anything about sitting down, or even standing still. Weaving prayer into everyday life means just that—praying while you do other things.

St. Paul said to "pray without ceasing." (1 Thessalonians 5:19) You may hear that message and figure that's all well and good for St. Paul 2,000 years ago, but it's not going to work for you today. Truth is, what St. Paul preached then is exactly what you're meant to work toward now. As you journey down this spiritual path, the eventual goal is to pray without ceasing, turning every action, every moment, your entire life into a prayer so you don't just say a prayer, you *become* the prayer. But it's not that easy getting from Point A to Point B. I know from experience.

I'm especially good at coming up with excuses for not praying, even when prayer time falls into my lap. At times, I allow myself to get caught in that *someday* trap, thinking there's a magical day down the road when all the planets will align and I will find myself with gobs of free time.

Prayer can be hard work, harder than cleaning or writing or doing your taxes, so we often manage to put it off and blame our circum-stances. "If only (*fill in the blank*), I'd be more holy."

But spending time with God isn't only about sitting down in silent prayer on a regular basis, although that's necessary as well. It's more often than not about learning to see your regular, boring, sometimes frustrating actions as prayers. You don't find God *after* all the work and other responsibilities are done; you find God *in* those responsibilities.

So toss out any notion that you're too busy to pray. Prayer is not going to be one more thing to add to the running tab of responsibilities you keep in the back of your mind, or hung by a magnet to the door of your fridge, or stored in an app on your smartphone. Rather than add to your stress level, prayer can become the thing that balances out all the other stresses and creates an oasis of calm in the middle of the mayhem.

Moving Meditation

Look at your prayer life right now. How do you pray? When do you pray? Consider adding a few minutes of prayer to the start of your day. Tape a favorite prayer or spiritual quote to your bathroom mirror and say the words—out loud or silently—as you shave or dry your hair. Or put a prayer in the kitchen where you'll see it as you make breakfast. I've got one prayer hanging above my makeup basket in my bathroom and another over my coffee maker in the kitchen. Because I'm not going anywhere without my morning coffee, I can rest assured I'll spot my prayer reminder and start my day off on the right spiritual foot.

MULTITASKING IS NOT A VIRTUE

I'm a champion multitasker. There was a time when I considered that a good thing, a sign I was working hard. After all, look at everything I had to do, everywhere I had to be, sometimes all at once. Surely my system overload was a sign of "success."

But multitasking quickly starts to take its toll. When you do six things at once, none of them are done with attention or intention. Everything becomes just a little haphazard—at least that's what I've found.

It's not unusual for me to carry around two phones and a laptop practically sparking from the number of simultaneous conversations going on Facebook, instant messenger, email, and Twitter. On a surface level alone, that kind of multitasking is sure to lead to a communications breakdown in one way or another—a message sent to the wrong person; a job sent before it's complete; a comment on someone's Facebook post that leads to tension, hard feelings, or even the ultimate social networking penalty, outright unfriending.

On a deeper level, however, that kind of fractured behavior leads to unrest and dissatisfaction deep within your soul. When nothing is ever done slowly and thoughtfully, let alone without interruption, you feel cheated of your peace, unable to stop the frenetic movement of your life. There never seems to be a resting place. Prayer can become that place, giving you the inner calm you crave and calling you back to a more focused and intentional way of living.

You may be wondering how it could possibly help to add the "task" of prayer to your daily routine. Seems like piling on. There is a danger that prayer can become just one more thing we multitask if we don't approach it with the right mind-set, but ultimately, true prayer is not a chore but a balm, not one more thing to do but the only thing that matters. Prayer won't take away the responsibilities and appointments that threaten to overwhelm you, but it will help you manage them with a sense of peace that pervades everything you do and allows you to face down your worst days with a sense of the sacred to ground you.

If you've ever been to the beach as the tide is going out, you've probably stood at the water's edge and felt the pull of the undertow as the water rushes back out to sea. If you stand perfectly still for just a few minutes, your feet begin to sink deeper and deeper into the sand. Despite the power of the crashing waves, you are grounded, strong, sure because your feet are firmly planted and surrounded by a support that won't let you fall.

Prayer is a lot like that. The more you pray, the deeper your roots sink into your foundation of faith, making you unshakable, unflappable even in the face of the biggest waves life sends your way.

Notes from the Journey

Logically, I can recognize the need to see Jesus in my children, my husband, my friends, my business colleagues, and even the lady holding up traffic at the drive-thru window at the bank. But practically speaking, it's a real challenge for me. Smiling my way through difficult things has never been my strong suit. Even as a young kid, my maternal grandmother would often scold me by saying, "Don't give me that look." Yes, I have a "look," an obvious expression of annoyance, frustration, disappointment— you name it. Mother Teresa I'm not. So the idea of giving up the look and the sarcasm that are a natural part of my personality for a serene smile is really not that appealing to me. Yet how do I become more centered, more God-focused if I let myself get carried away with the emotion of the day?

My challenge today will be to make the kids' breakfast with a prayerful heart, to calm my little one's crying with deep compassion rather than strong words, to paint the front door with patience even when the painter's tape fails, to meet my son's teen-aged glare with a smile rather than "the look." I know that kind of patience won't come through sheer willpower but through surrender to God. And surrender will only come through prayer. Today. Every day.

AN UNDERCURRENT OF MINDFULNESS

For many Catholics, the word *mindfulness* makes their ears perk up. Isn't that a Buddhist practice? What's it doing in a Catholic book on prayer?

Buddhism has long been associated with the slow and deliberate practice of mindfulness in all things—walking, eating, sweeping. But Catholic prayer, especially when it's woven into ordinary activities, requires that same mindfulness or single-minded attention.

"God is in the details," the popular saying goes. That's sort of the Catholic version of mindfulness. When you want to bring prayer into everyday life, you have to slow down and start noticing the details. The first step in this journey is awareness.

God is present in the mad dash to get the kids on the school bus, in the daffodil opening bit by bit with each spring day, in the vegetables you chop for your favorite soup, in the traffic jam that makes you late for work, in a song that inspires you to sing and dance. Wherever you are, God is there, if only you take the time to notice.

As you work your way through this book page by page, you will begin to peel back the surface stuff that distracts you from the Spirit at work in the most ordinary and seemingly unspiritual parts of your life. Mindfulness will be the constant throughout this prayer journey, and in becoming more mindful, you'll find that your penchant for multitasking begins to lessen. As prayerfulness and awareness take up residence in your core, the rush of the world will begin to lose some of its pull. Little by little, balance will be restored and you'll start to reclaim the inner peace you crave—and deserve.

A New Definition of Prayer

Not long ago, I gave a workshop on prayer for about 100 teenagers and their parents. I started my talk by asking the members of the audience to do a spiritual version of free association. "When I say the word *prayer*, what's the first thing that pops into your head?" I asked. No self-editing allowed. No second-guessing. Just spit it out.

After some initial blank stares, I heard the responses I expected: church, Hail Mary, kneeling, Our Father, quiet, candles, holy water, Sign of the Cross. And all those answers are correct, but they're just pieces of the larger fabric of Catholic prayer life. Ours is a rich and overflowing treasure chest of prayer styles and methods, with something to suit every personality and need.

For many of us, though, prayer has been relegated to a tiny box, something with defined boundaries, specific words, allocated time slots, and lots of rules. We remember having to memorize the classic prayers of our childhood, and to this day, the words to those prayers tumble out without effort, even if we aren't regular prayers.

Catholic prayer is so much more than that. Since the earliest days of our faith, prayer has been something meant to give rhythm to our days and years, something that can be specific or spontaneous, vocal or silent, said or sung. There's really no wrong way to pray if your intentions are good and you are open to the movement and guidance of the Spirit.

When you take prayer out of that box and unwrap all the beautiful and varied ways of speaking to God, you begin to realize that prayer does not require anything more from you than a willing heart. When asked about prayer, Blessed Pope John Paul II said in *The Way of Prayer*, "How to pray? This is a simple matter. I would say: Pray any way you like, so long as you do pray. You can pray the way your mother taught you; you can use a prayer book. Sometimes it takes courage to pray; but it is possible to pray, and necessary to pray, whether from memory or a book or just in thought, it is all the same."

And that's the heart of the matter. As soon as you feel that desire within to deepen your connection to the divine, as soon as you turn to face God, you have already begun to pray, no matter what words you say or whether you say anything at all.

As you enter into this everyday approach to prayer, you can use whatever prayer style best suits you. If that means saying the Hail Mary over and over, go for it. If it means staying in the silence of "mental" prayer, use that. If you prefer to pray for the needs of other people, known as "intercessory prayer," that's the perfect starting place. Pick and choose what works for you, but try not to close the door on a particular type of prayer. Your spiritual needs will change year by year, sometimes day by day, and what doesn't seem to work today may be the perfect method tomorrow. Just keep an open heart and an open mind.

Remember, too, that occasional but regular time set aside for prayer helps fortify you for everyday living and praying. Father Thomas Ryan, a Paulist priest I met at a prayer workshop, compares such prayer to soaking a sponge. You need to soak a sponge to clean a dirty counter; if you try to clean with a dry sponge, not much is going to happen, he explains. And so it is with prayer. If you try to pray in the everyday without ever going back to the well to be soaked by the graces that come from things like Scripture, Mass, Eucharist, private devotions, meditation, and more, you won't be able to get that below-the-surface "dirt" life puts in front of you.

INFORMATION OVERLOAD

One of the great things of living in the internet era is the immediate and around-the-clock access to information on every topic imaginable. That also happens to be one of the worst things about living in the internet era. You can Google any subject, quote, snippet of song, philosophy, spirituality, diet, history, news story, and more. And while that may be great for people writing research papers, it can become just one more distraction if you're hoping to deepen your prayer life. Rather than pray, you may search for information on prayer, imagining you'll read yourself to eternal salvation, gathering up every last pointer.

But prayer is as individual as a fingerprint. The way you pray, and your connection to God, is yours alone. While you can gain insights and direction from those who have been down this road before, if you wait until you know everything there is to know about prayer, you'll never begin.

Just do it, as the Nike commercial says. Start praying now. It's good to read and research to add depth to your practice and to explore new methods, but don't let that keep you from beginning right where you are.

BECOMING COUNTERCULTURAL

Everyday prayerfulness and mindfulness show us a way of living that runs counter to everything the world around us says.

Bringing prayer into everyday life requires that you go against the grain, become "countercultural." It means slowing down when the rest of the world is moving at warp speed. It means doing one thing at a time in a world that views anything less than constant multi-tasking as lazy or unmotivated. It means saying "No" every once in a while because you recognize that agreeing to one more project, one more volunteer responsibility, one more commitment means you become less whole and more fragmented.

Just know in your heart that this way of mindfulness, this path that leads you ever closer to God, brings a sense of sanity and serenity to your life few people even realize is possible anymore.

Practical Wisdom

One of the things you can do is remember all during the day that God is with you ... We can present our souls to him a thousand times a day. Sprinkle a seasoning of short prayers into your daily living. If you see something beautiful, thank God for it. If you are aware of someone's need, ask God to help.

—St. Francis de Sales, *The Devout Life*

THE GRACE TO BE A BEGINNER

Whenever you undertake a new skill, or even a more advanced level of a familiar skill, you probably recognize at the outset that it's going to require practice. Lots of it. Whether you're learning to play piano for the first time or brushing up on your Spanish pronunciation for an upcoming trip, there's no way you can go from zero to sixty without regular time devoted to study and practice.

So why is it that we so often expect to be experts in prayer without any effort at all? You show up in prayer and feel frustrated when your mind wanders, when your back gets tired from sitting or kneeling so straight, when the words come but the feeling of something deeper is missing.

Although the beginning of a prayer practice is, as I mentioned earlier, as simple and "easy" as showing up before God with an open heart, if you want to move forward toward deeper and deeper connection and contemplation, you're going to have to give yourself a chance to stumble a bit, a chance to feel your way around as you figure out where to go next. In other words, you have to give yourself the permission to be a beginner, and that's not always easy in this world where being the best at everything you do is the only acceptable option.

Notes from the Journey

I'm not good at being a beginner. I want to be an expert from Day 1. No matter what I'm doing. Even when I'm doing something I've never done before. Not sure where that mentality comes from, but it's a stumbling block. To expect perfection in everything is a surefire path to "failure," or to not trying at all.

I need the willingness to be a beginner in prayer, to sit there and be open to whatever might unfold, to come back day after day even when it feels like I'm not progressing and just practice my "craft," the craft of praying.

This week in the early morning hours before anyone else is awake, I've been saying Morning Prayer out on the deck or in my sun porch. And slowly, slowly I have found a rhythm there that feels right, one I hope I can keep up for good. As soon as that thought enters my mind, I realize I'm heading right back to the quest for perfection instead of living in this moment, praying in this moment, one day at a time.

Often coupled with the unwillingness to be a beginner at prayer, or anything else, is a quest for perfection. You start to pray and immediately expect some sort of momentous confirmation of your abilities—choirs of angels singing, undeniable answers of "Yes!" to your heart's desires, a sudden and deep sense of peace where before there was only stress and chaos. But prayer doesn't work that way.

Even when you show up in prayer day after day, week after week, you're not going to find perfection. You may experience "progress," according to the human desire to mark your climb up the spiritual ladder, but even that is off base. Practice makes you more open. Practice leads you closer to God, closer to your true self, and closer to others, but it won't necessarily make you a perfect pray-er. Even the greatest saints had difficulties in their prayer lives, moments when they felt nothing. Days, months, years where they felt no "progress."

The whole practice-makes-perfect mentality doesn't belong in prayer life. Remember, it's okay to be a beginner. Better than okay, in fact. Revel in being a beginner. Understand that you will move forward and maybe even feel a divine connection some days; other days your prayers may feel empty. In spiritual life, your motto should be "Practice makes perfect sense but not perfect prayer." God accepts you in prayer just as you are; perfection is never a condition.

Moving Meditation

Practice being a beginner today. Find one prayer method you've never tried before or something you've tried but quit because you didn't think you were good enough, and simply begin. No long-range goals, no image of perfection. Try a few minutes of silent prayer sitting in your living room looking out the window, or go for a walk around the block while you say a decade of the Rosary. Whatever you choose, just begin and see what wonderful and unexpected places it takes you when you don't have any preconceived ideas about where you "should" be.

TWO STEPS FORWARD

I wish I could promise you that with the background and suggestions in this book and a little effort on your part, you'll soar through spiritual life like a super saint, but prayer, like just about everything else in life, does not proceed in a straight line.

You will get sidetracked and thrown totally off course now and then. You'll get into a daily rhythm that feels like it will go on and on for the rest of your life, only to hit a setback due to sickness or work or family or any number of outside situations. Even everyday prayer can hit a snag sometimes.

Perseverance is the key. If you return to your practices again and again—even if you fall off the wagon, so to speak—you'll keep moving in the right direction.

Prayer practice can be a lot like dieting or physical exercise. You may go through periods when all engines are firing and you're moving with certainty and at warp speed and then something gets in your way and suddenly you trip, slow down, or quit. When you hit those patches, you have to get back up and try again. You may need to experiment with a new type of prayer or change the ways you're including it in your daily routine. Sometimes you can get a little too comfortable, and you need to switch things up to keep your spiritual muscles engaged.

Endless options can help you keep your spiritual life on track and moving forward; take advantage of all of them. It may be a dance of two steps forward and one step back, but you'll still be inching closer toward God with every prayer.

MAKING PRAYER NON-NEGOTIABLE

When it comes to your personal life and spiritual health, everything, it seems, is up for grabs. You have a crushing deadline approaching at the office, so you cut out Evening Prayer to stay late and get some extra work done. The kids are home from school with strep throat, so you skip the afternoon meditation you had planned. The bathrooms need to be cleaned, so you cross daily Mass off the list of things you had hoped to do and grab the toilet brush instead.

But when life gets overloaded and stressful, prayer should be the *last* thing to go, not the first. That's when you need prayer most. Remember the beach scene with the tide rushing out? If you drop prayer from your life when things get a little stormy, you're going to be carried out to sea by whatever crisis pops up.

Begin to see prayer as something vital, like eating or breathing. In a way, it's a lot like those essential basics, providing nourishment and lifeblood for your soul. Decide at the outset of this prayer journey that your spiritual practice has value beyond anything the world can see or understand and then make a promise to stick with your plan, no matter what.

The good news is that there's really no good reason to skip everyday prayer. Maybe you don't have time to sit and meditate, but you always have time to pray as you drive, as you cook, as you eat lunch, or as you wait in the car line outside school in the afternoon.

GETTING STARTED

You may want to have a few things on hand as you begin this journey. I recommend having a Bible nearby so you can look up full versions of passages you may find here or to offer fuel for spiritual reflection. In addition, a notebook or journal is a good idea. It can be helpful to jot down things that speak to you—a quote or passage, a prayer tip, an experience that made you aware of the Spirit moving in your life.

If you have other favorite prayer aids, keep them with this book and your journal as well—a prayer card of a favorite saint, your Rosary beads, a CD of sacred music, or whatever inspires you in prayer.

Any prayers mentioned in the chapters that follow are included in Appendix A at the back of the book. So if you see something that sounds unfamiliar or something you'd like to explore further, just check the appendix.

All you absolutely need right now, however, is an open heart and a willing spirit. God is already waiting for you, longing for you. Just turn your thoughts and mind in God's direction, and your spiritual journey has begun.

Practical Wisdom

For me, prayer is a surge of the heart; it is a simple look turned toward heaven, it is a cry of recognition and of love, embracing both trial and joy.
—St. Thérèse of Lisieux

GOING FORWARD ...

† Start to cultivate awareness and mindfulness in everyday life. Pay attention to the details of your days.

† Be willing to be a beginner when it comes to prayer. Practice often, but don't expect perfection.

† Even the saints experienced difficulty in prayer. When you hit a rough patch, remember you are not alone.

† Make prayer non-negotiable. See it as a vital part of keeping life in balance.

† Notice how even a few minutes of daily prayer begin to transform your attitude, your actions, and your life.

2

BUILDING A SPIRITUAL FOUNDATION

It's not uncommon, when you decide to pray in the everyday moments of your life, to find yourself at a loss for words. You want to pray as you commute to work, but what prayer should you use? You're aching to try the Rosary as you walk, but you still don't have the mysteries memorized. You've heard that praying the Liturgy of the Hours is a perfect way to link your daily prayers with those of the larger Church, but where do you even begin?

You're not alone. Not by a long shot. Even the apostles, the guys who traveled around with the Son of God on a day-to-day basis, finally had to come right out and ask: "Lord, teach us to pray."

Deciding to pray is one thing. Coming up with specific prayer practices built around certain words and methods can be a little overwhelming.

You've probably got far more prayer knowledge built up in your head and your heart than you even realize. The basic prayers—Sign of the Cross, Hail Mary, Our Father, Glory Be—are most likely part of your spiritual DNA, the words spilling out effortlessly and on cue. You may even be adept at many of the more intricate prayer forms of the Catholic faith, and yet figuring out how to fit those traditional prayers into nontraditional settings can be a challenge at times.

When it comes to Catholic prayer options, there really is something for everyone, which can be both good and bad—so many prayers, so little time. Take a look at the basic rundown in this chapter.

Whether the following pages serve as a brief refresher course or a step-by-step how-to guide, I hope you'll be able to come away with something new, something you can apply to the everyday prayer opportunities you'll discover in the chapters ahead.

A Few Prayer Essentials

Prayers tend to fall into one of a few general categories: petition, intercession, thanksgiving, praise, and adoration. Even basic prayers, like the Our Father, include elements of these kinds of prayer within them.

Petitions

Probably the most common thing you—and pretty much all pray-ers—do when praying is ask for God's help in one way or another. You may go to God with "petitions," or requests for specific things, from the healing of a terrible illness, to the sale of a home, to the end of an addiction, to good weather for your vacation. There's no need too great or too small that doesn't get put before God at one point or another.

I seem to talk to God in an ongoing conversation punctuated by petitions, but I take comfort in the fact that Jesus told his followers, "Ask and it will be given to you; seek and you will find; knock and the door will be opened to you." (Matthew 7:7)

In the "Parable of the Persistent Widow," Jesus likens our prayer efforts to the woman who keeps going back to a dishonest judge to ask him to render a just decision in a case. The judge eventually hears her, not because she wins him over with her arguments but because she wears him down with her persistence. "Will not God then secure the rights of his chosen ones who call out to him day and night?" Jesus asks, reminding his followers in not so many words that they should basically drive God crazy with petitions and prayer needs. (Luke 18:1–8)

INTERCESSIONS

When you say a prayer of petition on behalf of someone else, it becomes an "intercession." You're asking God to answer someone else's prayer. Sometimes you may also go to Mary and the saints and ask them to intercede (to serve as a middle man, so to speak) for you, for your loved ones and friends, even for strangers a world away. Intercessory prayer can be a powerful practice, especially when coupled with everyday activities, as you'll see in the pages to come.

Whenever I find myself at a loss for words or with inability to sit in silent stillness, I default to intercessory prayer. Praying for other people shifts my focus away from my own needs, desires, complaints, and onto those who could truly use some spiritual or even physical help.

Practical Wisdom

Pray inwardly, even if you do not enjoy it. It does good, though you feel nothing; yes, even though you think you are doing nothing.

—Julian of Norwich, fourteenth-century mystic

THANKSGIVING

Prayers of thanksgiving or gratitude also tend to be pretty high up on the popular prayer list. If you're not asking for something, you're probably saying thank you for something, which is a good thing.

Expressing thanks to God for prayers answered is likely to make you even more grateful for everything else in your life, the not-so-good along with the good. Gratitude has the power to transform, so keep that in mind as you pick and choose your practices in the days ahead.

PRAISE

When you step outside prayers of petition and thanksgiving to simply celebrate God's goodness—no strings attached—you've got prayers of praise.

These prayers aren't used as easily and as often as the others simply because human needs always seem to be at the fore. Praise is a chance to get away from the asking and thanking and focus directly on God's love and generosity.

ADORATION

Take that one step further, and you've got adoration. In this type of prayer, you're not just praising God, you are *exalting* him, as we hear so often in the psalms: "I will extol you, my God and king; I will bless your name forever. Every day will I bless you; I will praise your name forever. Great is the Lord and worthy of high praise. God's grandeur is beyond understanding." (Psalm 145:1–4)

Adoration also refers to a specific type of prayer before the Blessed Sacrament, or Eucharist, either in church during monthly, weekly, or perhaps even perpetual adoration "events" or before the Blessed Sacrament in the tabernacle on any day of the week. Some people sit quietly before the tabernacle and simply reflect in God's presence; others say the Rosary; still others read Scripture or pray the Liturgy of the Hours during periods of adoration.

Although this is less likely to be part of an everyday prayer routine, if you can pop into a local church now and then and make "a visit," you'll get a little fortification for the journey ahead and a whole bunch of spiritual graces. Even if you have no idea what to do when you get there, give it a shot. Simply sit before the Lord and wait in silent wonder at the immense gift before you.

BLESSINGS

Blessings aren't typically included in this particular category or prayer—they're known as "sacramentals," something I'll cover later—but they are common choices as we go about our daily life. Grace before meals, a blessing whispered over a new baby, the blessing of an Advent wreath or new home—these are prayers that give God praise while asking that he send down his protection and blessings.

You may think only priests can offer blessings, but take heart: you, too, can shower blessings upon your household and the people you love.

Moving Meditation

Start a gratitude journal. Every day, take note of the things for which you are thankful. It doesn't have to be something monumental. It could be the full moon that caught you by surprise as you drove home, the sound of your children giggling in another room, or the smell of muffins baking in the morning. By noticing the many little blessings in your life, you'll start to shift your spiritual perspective in dramatic ways.

MASS AS PRIMARY SOURCE

For Catholics, no prayer is as great or as significant as the Mass. This is the high point of prayer life because this is the prayer that feeds all the others.

As I suggested in the previous chapter, to effectively and continually weave prayer into your daily activities, you need to go back to the well regularly to soak yourself in the refreshing waters of God's word and nourish yourself at the table of the Lord.

Unless you're a priest or you live very close to a parish with daily Eucharistic celebrations, weekday Mass might not be an option for you. Still, it's important to get to Mass as often as you can, and at least on Sundays. Without the liturgy and Eucharist to sustain you, daily prayer becomes more difficult. You need to load up on spiritual sustenance for the days ahead in much the same way you'd load up on carbs before running a marathon.

CELEBRATING EUCHARIST

The centerpiece of the Mass and of Catholic faith life is, of course, the Eucharist. This spiritual time and food is meant to give you strength and peace and comfort, while also challenging you to share those gifts to those around you, to bring Jesus' message of love and mercy to everyone you meet.

At the Last Supper, when Jesus knew his time had come, he wanted to leave his followers with something to sustain them. In the form of bread and wine, Jesus gave his disciples then and us today the gift of his Body and Blood, a memorial of his death and resurrection, a physical and lasting connection to God. This spiritual food gives us the grace to go on, direction when we're lost, and courage when we're foundering.

It's easy to get caught up in a mistaken view of Eucharist, or Communion, as punishment or reward. At least I find myself fighting that feeling at times. If I've had a bad week, if my prayer life has been in the doldrums, if I've felt like a failure at motherhood or marriage or life in general, I sometimes feel I should hang back and skip Communion, thinking I'm not in the right place mentally or spiritually to receive Jesus. And yet that's the exact right place and time to run to Jesus and receive him in Communion.

Yes, you are meant to be in a "state of grace" when you receive Communion, meaning you have no serious sin hanging over you, but you are not meant to be perfect or without fault. Through the Eucharist, you get what you need to move forward and overcome your weaknesses, so try to get to Mass as often as you can.

STRENGTH IN COMMUNITY

You never have to go it alone in Catholic spirituality. In fact, you're not meant to make this journey by yourself. Jesus clearly understood that, having sent his disciples out in pairs. He knew they'd need spiritual friends to help them through the rough patches, to pray with them and for them, to be companions on the path to heaven.

Spiritual life is meant to be a shared journey, which is why Mass is such a critical part of Catholic life. In addition to the nourishment and graces received through Eucharist, the community experience of Mass is vital to spiritual growth. "For where two or three are gathered together in my name, there am I in the midst of them," Jesus said. (Matthew 18:20)

It's important to have an individual and private prayer life, but it's equally important to come together with your brothers and sisters in faith to praise God together and share a spiritual meal. It's in your faith community that you find friends to walk with you. If you haven't already made some connections in your local parish, begin to join organizations, attend events, and introduce yourself to fellow parishioners.

In the earliest days of the Christian faith, Jesus' followers lived together, ate together, prayed together, and shared all their possessions. Their life in Christ was not separate from their life in general. Although our Church has grown too big for that kind of constant communal living, Catholics have an opportunity every week, every day to come together and spend time in prayer with like-minded pilgrims on the spiritual path.

Community is critical to faith life, so even if you're working hard to pray in the ordinary moments of your private life, be sure to take advantage of the many opportunities to pray with others.

Notes from the Journey

Working from home can sometimes feed into my tendency to be hermit-like in my prayer life. In my basement office, with incense burning and meditative music playing, it's easy to feel as though I don't need anything more than me, myself, and I.

I sit in my prayer space and pray, sometimes silently, other times out loud. Why search for God anywhere else? I can make my connection to the divine without leaving the house, without changing out of my sweatpants.

But today I decided to venture out to 12:15 P.M. Mass at my parish. I walked into the small but crowded chapel and took my seat, still not sure if I really needed this midday Monday break. A few people I know waved or nodded from their seats across the room.

The readings that day resonated powerfully with me, as is so often the case when I go to Mass. I felt as if the message was written specifically for me. By the time I went up to receive Communion, I knew I was supposed to be in church that day. I needed it.

After Mass, several people I haven't seen in a while came over to talk with me, asking about my work projects, my health, my family. There in our parish gathering space I was reminded, once again, that sometimes I need to break out of my basement routine and seek support and encouragement from fellow travelers on the journey.

PRIVATE DEVOTIONS

For most Catholics, certain prayers are staples. Even if they don't say them often, they know them or know *of* them. The treasury of Catholic prayers is almost endless.

In addition to the Rosary, probably the most well-known of Catholic devotions, there are novenas, chaplets, litanies, and prayers to the angels and saints. All are available to you as part of everyday prayer life. Some are more easily suited to busyness, and others to silence or solitude, but they are all beautiful methods of growing closer to God and finding the deep-seated peace and serenity you crave.

THE ROSARY

I don't know how many sets of Rosary beads I have jangling around my house, but it's probably too many to count. I have a bunch in my nightstand drawer, one in my office, and several blessed by the pope and brought home from Rome only to sit in my closet. Even my youngest child has a Rosary collection hanging from her doorknob, a noisy reminder of this meditative prayer form.

I wish I could say we used our Rosaries regularly, but I've always felt I was Rosary challenged. I struggle with this popular and basic Catholic devotion, which on the surface seems to be about the Blessed Mother but is actually a meditation on the life of Christ.

"With the Rosary, the Christian people *sits at the school of Mary* and is led to contemplate the beauty on the face of Christ and to experience the depths of his love," Blessed Pope John Paul II wrote in his 2002 Apostolic Letter *Rosarium Virginis Mariae*. "Through the Rosary the faithful receive abundant grace, as though from the very hands of the Mother of the Redeemer."

By using the most basic prayers of the faith—the Our Father, Hail Mary, Glory Be, and Apostles' Creed—you can work your way around the beads, spending a little time focusing on a different "mystery" for each of the five decades.

There are four categories of mysteries: joyful, luminous, sorrowful, and glorious. Each set focuses on different aspects of Jesus' life, with Mary ever-present not only in the words of the prayers but in the scenes for many of the meditations. (For a full explanation of the mysteries and instructions on how to pray the Rosary, see Appendix A.)

Here's a brief breakdown of the mysteries:

The joyful mysteries include the Annunciation, Visitation, Nativity, Presentation in the Temple, and Finding of the Child Jesus.

The luminous mysteries, which were added to the Rosary by Blessed Pope John Paul II in 2002, include Jesus' Baptism in the Jordan, the Wedding at Cana, the Proclamation of the Kingdom of God, the Transfiguration, and the Institution of the Eucharist.

The sorrowful mysteries include the Agony in the Garden, the Scourging at the Pillar, the Crowning with Thorns, the Carrying of the Cross, and the Crucifixion.

And the glorious mysteries include the Resurrection, the Ascension of our Lord, the Descent of the Holy Spirit, the Assumption of Mary into Heaven, and the Crowning of Mary.

Those who pray the Rosary regularly typically pray certain mysteries on certain days: joyful on Monday and Saturday; luminous on Thursday; sorrowful on Tuesday and Friday; and glorious on Wednesday and Sunday.

"To pray the Rosary is to hand over our burdens to the merciful hearts of Christ and his Mother," wrote Blessed Pope John Paul II, who called the Rosary a "compendium" of the Gospel. "… the Rosary does indeed 'mark the rhythm of human life,' bringing it into harmony with the 'rhythm' of God's own life, in the joyful communion of the Holy Trinity, our life's destiny and deepest longing."

Given its popularity and familiarity—not to mention its focus on the Blessed Mother, a perennial favorite among Catholics—the Rosary is one of the most common devotions for those who pray in the everyday. Time and again, when I asked people how they wove prayer into everyday life, they cited the Rosary as their go-to. Some used it while walking, some while driving, some while doing laundry, some while gardening. As you'll see in the chapters to come, the rhythm of certain prayers, like the Rosary, are a perfect complement to the rhythm of certain daily actions, like walking or driving.

Practical Wisdom

There is no right way to pray the Rosary. It is like a thread that runs through our lives. The thread is not so much the beads themselves, or even the specific prayers … it is the Word of God, the Scripture, that is the thread tied on one end to us and the other end to God.

—Megan McKenna, *Praying the Rosary*

NOVENAS AND OTHER OPTIONS

When I was a kid, my mother would take me over to church every Monday night for a novena, which literally means "nine"—a novena is a prayer said on nine consecutive days or nine consecutive Mondays or whatever schedule of nine you're using. Novenas have a specific focus—Sacred Heart, Immaculate Heart, St. Jude—and are said in hopes of receiving special graces and perhaps the answer to a particular prayer. Although not as popular among the faithful today, novenas are another Catholic prayer option for those looking to expand their spiritual repertoire.

2 Building a Spiritual Foundation   27

You can also pray a "chaplet," which is prayed on beads and some-times even employs Rosary beads while saying different prayers. A currently popular chaplet is the Divine Mercy Chaplet, which is said at 3 P.M. every day.

When I was in Rome a few years ago, I was walking around in search of some lunch with a couple other Catholic journalists. As we started out, a clock somewhere chimed 3, and my two colleagues took out their Rosary beads and began to say the prayers of the Divine Mercy Chaplet, something I had never prayed before.

As we wove our way through twisting, narrow, cobblestone streets, we prayed, all the while dodging Vespas, checking maps, and hiking up ancient pathways in our quest for some pasta and wine. If ever I needed a reminder that you can always pray in the everyday, that was it. As I tried to keep up—both physically and prayerfully—I felt a sense of calm despite the noise and heat and occasional wrong turn.

SAINTS AND ANGELS

You may have one or two favorite saints. St. Francis of Assisi, St. Anthony, and St. Jude are often likely candidates, as is St. Thérèse and a host of other spiritual notables, especially such up-and-coming saints as Blessed Mother Teresa and Blessed Pope John Paul II. These holy men and women serve as wonderful spiritual role models, and their writings can often provide serious fodder for the spiritual gristmill.

Explore the lives of the saints. Find some that speak to you through their words, their actions, their histories, or their outlooks. When-ever you need some inspiration for prayer life, you're sure to find it among the saints, whose backgrounds run the gamut, from popes and bishops to housewives and carpenters. (Check Appendix A for some specific prayers associated with the saints.)

Angels are also popular in Catholic prayer. Catholics believe that every soul that comes into the world has a guardian angel, a being who offers protection and guidance for life. Angels are not to be confused with the souls of those who have died. Angels are purely spiritual, never having had earthly bodies.

You can find angel references throughout the Scriptures, from key moments of Hebrew Scripture to some of the most "famous" scenes of Christian Scripture—the angel Gabriel coming to Mary to tell she has been chosen to bear God's Son, and the angel in the field announcing the birth of a Savior.

I grew up saying the Angel of God prayer every night before bed. My angel connection dimmed for a while; I guess I thought I had outgrown them. But in recent years, I have found myself drawn to the angels once again. Although I do, on occasion, ask for protection and guidance from my own guardian angel, more often than not I'm praying that the guardian angels of my children be on high alert as my kids begin—with increasing frequency—to venture out from under my watchful eyes.

Practical Wisdom

We cannot pass our guardian angel's bounds, resigned or sullen, he will hear our sighs.

—St. Augustine

Ancient Traditions

From its beginning, the Christian faith has been rich in prayer methods that spring from our Hebrew roots and the faith practices of Jesus' earliest followers. Using Scripture, praying at certain hours, marking the seasons, making spiritual pilgrimages, and other ancient methods can bring a spiritual rhythm and sense of the sacred to modern life.

The Liturgy of the Hours

Known as the "prayer of the Church," the Liturgy of the Hours, or Divine Office, is a prayer that does just what it says: it marks the hours of the day. Rooted in Jewish tradition and developed by the earliest monastic communities and clergy, this prayer remains a centerpiece of Catholic prayer life, although up until recent years, it was said mainly by priests and those living in religious communities.

Now, however, increasing numbers of lay Catholics are seeking out this prayer, which revolves around the psalms and canticles and also includes hymns, Scripture readings, prayers of intercession, and the Our Father.

Morning Prayer and Evening Prayer are considered the "hinges" of the day, making them the most critical of the hours. To pray the full Liturgy of the Hours, however, you would have to get up in the early morning, say around 2 A.M., to pray the Office of Readings, also known as Matins or Vigils. You would say Morning Prayer around 6 A.M., followed by Mid-Morning Prayer at 9 A.M., Midday Prayer around 11 A.M., Mid-Afternoon Prayer around 3 P.M., Evening Prayer around 5 P.M., and Night Prayer or Compline at 7 P.M. That schedule is all well and good if you live in a monastery or hermitage, but if you, like me, live in a busy house, praying the Hours in full can become an exercise in frustration.

If you decide you want to try this prayer, find a community, such as a nearby monastery or convent or a local church, that will let you join them in saying it until you learn the ropes. It's easier to learn if you have someone to guide you. Check Appendix A for some basic instructions for praying the Hours, or go to Appendix C for books or apps that can take you further into the practice.

If you can do Morning and Evening Prayer—or maybe Morning Prayer and Compline, since 5 P.M. Evening Prayer isn't exactly convenient for most working people or busy families—you'll begin to see how the Hours can bring a certain sacred rhythm to your day and your life.

PRAYING WITH SCRIPTURE

Even if you don't say the Liturgy of the Hours, you may like the idea of weaving Scripture into your everyday prayer life. You can do as little or as much as you'd like.

Start simple. Look up the readings for the day, or maybe a favorite passage, and simply read that. Read it again and see if anything specific speaks to you. If something jumps out at you, roll it around in your mind and pray on it. Talk to God and then wait to see if he is trying to tell you anything. This is basically a simplified form of what's known as *Lectio Divina*, which means "sacred reading."

Scripture really is at the center of so many different Catholic prayer practices, from the Mass, the Rosary, and the Liturgy of the Hours, to the words of the Hail Mary, taken from the Gospel of Luke, and the words of the Our Father, which has been called a summary of the Gospel.

Moving Meditation

Get into the habit of reading Sunday's Gospel ahead of time as a way to enter more fully into Mass each week. You can find the cycle of readings in a printed missal, online, or even on apps for your smartphone. (See Appendix C.) Read the Gospel early in the week. Maybe even read it each day. Find lines that stand out to you or thoughts that come up when you read it. Reflect on those as you go about your daily activities. When you go to Mass, your familiarity with the Gospel reading will allow you to sink deeper into the word and find insights you otherwise might have missed.

BRIEF BUT POWERFUL

Prayer never needs to be complicated, but that doesn't mean it still can't be profound. Sometimes in seemingly simple words, you can convey deep spiritual truths.

The Jesus Prayer is one of the most ancient prayer practices in Christian tradition and is still used regularly by those in the Eastern Rite Church. It is a one-line prayer:

> Lord Jesus Christ, Son of God, have mercy on
> me, a sinner.

These few words express so much, making this a powerful prayer for those looking to pray without ceasing.

You start by saying the prayer aloud and progress to saying it quietly, to saying it silently, to simply thinking it, to allowing your life to become it. When said over and over, like a mantra of sorts, the prayer infuses every element of your daily life with the power of faith in Jesus Christ. If you can't do it without ceasing, at least try it now and then or at specific times that work for you.

Other simple prayers, often known as "aspirations," can be used the same way. Those who pray to the Divine Mercy often say this:

> Jesus, I trust in you.

When I was growing up, I remember my grandmother saying, "Jesus, Mary, and Joseph, I love you. Save souls." To this day, when I hear those words, I think of her and her way of praying without ceasing. Here are some other aspirations to consider:

> My Lord and my God.
>
> Praise be Jesus Christ, now and forevermore.
>
> Come, Holy Spirit.

When you can't think of anything else to say or don't have time to say longer prayers, use a one-line aspiration to keep your spiritual connection alive.

INTERIOR PRAYER

Although it's not necessarily easy to weave deep silent prayer into busy modern life, it's still important to find those moments of quiet whenever and wherever you can.

Meditation, which is so often considered exclusive to Eastern spirituality, is very much a part of Catholic prayer life and has been since its earliest beginnings. Unlike Eastern meditation, the Catholic version of this prayer style is not an attempt to empty the mind but instead to *focus* the mind—on a Scripture passage, an image such as an icon, or some other spiritual prompt—to bring you closer and closer to Christ.

Contemplation is a deeper form of silent prayer, one that's totally inward moving. In this prayer form, you "rest" in God, letting your interior gaze settle on Jesus, all the while allowing the Spirit to guide your heart and mind.

These silent prayer methods take some practice and some time set aside from everyday activities, but they are vital to spiritual growth and personal satisfaction. Begin to explore small moments of silence here and there, and see how just a few minutes can calm your soul and redirect your negative energy. I talk more about this style of prayer in Chapter 7.

Practical Wisdom

God is a friend of silence.
—Blessed Mother Teresa of Calcutta

GOING FORWARD …

† The Catholic treasury of prayer is so vast there really is something for everyone. Pick a style that suits you.

† Fall back on some prayer basics when you're struggling to pray in the everyday.

† Go to Mass and receive Communion as often as possible to help sustain you on your spiritual journey.

† Explore or revisit some private devotions and ancient traditions to boost your spiritual life.

† Silent, interior prayer may not be possible amid everyday busyness, but finding even a few minutes of quiet time each day can be transforming.

3

Turning Chores into Spiritual Practice

When I walk into my kitchen and see the sink piled with dirty dishes and the counter cluttered with yesterday's junk mail, prayer isn't usually the first thing that comes to mind. Mostly, I feel a bit suffocated, wishing I could climb out from under the household chores that require my attention day after day, an endless loop of washing and folding, scrubbing and straightening, weeding and raking that restore order to my home even if they can't restore order to my soul.

Or can they?

Minding the Mundane

Not long ago, I was fighting a silent battle with my family over the mountains of laundry I move up and down two flights of stairs, from bedrooms to basement, dragging hampers and baskets from room to room with an assortment of dirty (and eventually clean) jeans and sweatshirts, dance outfits and soccer uniforms, pajamas and socks. It got to the point where the laundry really had the power to ruin an otherwise perfectly good day.

To say that the laundry had become a spiritual albatross around my neck really isn't much of an exaggeration. Any peace I had found in silent meditation earlier in the day would vanish as quickly as the wisp of smoke from my recently extinguished prayer candle. Even as I sat in bed at night reading spiritual reflections, my mind would be churning with resentment over the laundry basket in view whenever I peered over the top of my book.

Then I remembered something Blessed Mother Teresa once said. We are not all called to do great things but to do "ordinary things with extraordinary love." And what could be more ordinary than doing the laundry? So I decided to put her message into practice, and rather than view the laundry as the thing taking me away from my quiet time, see it instead as an entry point, a way to pray—and love—even as I worked.

Where I once grumbled under my breath, I whispered short vocal prayers. I'd pick up my tween daughter's "skinny jeans" and say, "For Olivia. Help her to stay on right paths and make good choices. Hail Mary, full of grace ...." With a pair of socks, I'd turn my thoughts and prayers to my son, and so on, making every article of clothing an opportunity to express my love for my family, not necessarily in big, bold ways they'd notice but in small and, quite possibly, "extraordinary" ways that mattered more.

The prayer practice has transformed a dreaded chore into something truly positive and deeply spiritual for me. Even when I'm somewhat harried, tossing darks into one bin and lights into another, even when I'm verging on backsliding into resentment, the awareness created by my practice catches me. I will pick up a tiny black velvet dance outfit and settle my thoughts on my young daughter's sweet countenance, or I'll check the pockets of my teen son's jacket and recognize there, among the spare change and ballpoint pens, the harsh reality of how quickly life is moving and how easily we get sidetracked into discontent when we are blessed and graced and given more than should ever reasonably be expected of a simple life.

Practical Wisdom

Today we are not content with little achievements, with small beginnings. We should look to St. Teresa, the Little Flower, to walk her little way, her way of love. We should look to St. Teresa of Avila, who was not content to be like those people who proceeded with the pace of hens about God's business, but like those people who on their own account were greatly daring in what they wished to do for God.

—Dorothy Day, founder of the Catholic Worker Movement

THE LITTLE WAY

Despite how it often appears on the surface, daily life, even at its busiest, is ripe with prayer potential. This kind of spirituality of the ordinary is closely associated with St. Thérèse of Lisieux, the nineteenth-century Carmelite nun who is known for her "Little Way," a deceptively simple approach to prayer.

When I was younger, I didn't put much stock in St. Thérèse, who is known as the "Little Flower." Her nickname and her spirituality seemed, well, too little. I wanted big changes, big plans, big results. Her focus on all things "little" made her seem like a bit of a saintly shrinking violet. Then I picked up her autobiography, *The Story of a Soul*, which is considered a spiritual classic, and realized that the willingness to be little, to find grace in the miniscule moments of daily life, is actually the much harder but more satisfying path to walk.

"I realized that if every tiny flower wanted to be a rose, spring would lose its loveliness and there would be no wild flowers to make the meadows gay …. The sun shines equally both on cedars and on every tiny flower. In just the same way God looks after every soul as if it had no equal," St. Thérèse wrote, giving us a glimpse into the thinking that led to her Little Way.

Later in her book, St. Thérèse talks about the simplicity of the soul and how the closer we get to God, the simpler our souls become, reminding us that our spiritual journey isn't one of racking up "accomplishments" or even making great strides. We are at our spiritual best when we let all those goals fall away and we become childlike in our love for God and others.

"The little way is the way of spiritual childhood: the way of trust and of entire self-surrender," St. Thérèse wrote.

When my dear friend Dorothy Armstrong visited last summer, she would say with absolute joy in her voice, "My Father made that!" every time she saw something beautiful—a flower blossoming along a wooded path, a bounty of vegetables at the farmers' market, a yellow jacket buzzing too close for comfort on our back deck. My young daughters would look at her like she was slightly nuts, at first not realizing that when she referred to "her Father," she was referring to God and not her biological father. The familiarity in her voice made them wonder whether she could possibly be talking about God in such a way. Eventually they caught on, but it sure did take them by surprise.

That kind of childlike joy in God's goodness has been one of Dorothy's calling cards since I first met her almost 30 years ago, back when I was just out of college and she was nearing 50. We worked in the same building, and I would often sneak off to her office when I needed a little sanity or joy in the middle of a particularly rough work day. All these years later, a call or visit to Dorothy, who had been a cloistered nun before I knew her, brings that joy rushing back, filling me with a real sense of what it means to live in God's light, to walk the Little Way.

THE HABIT OF PRAYER

Dorothy has a daily prayer practice that keeps her connected to God even as she goes about the business of her day. Each day of the week, she focuses her prayers on specific intentions. For example, on Mondays she prays the Rosary for "working people," especially those who hate their jobs or those who have to drive long distances to get to work. She links each one of the joyful mysteries to a different group of workers—teachers, managers, those who are unemployed or "lost," nursing home workers, and on and on. On Tuesdays, she prays for her immediate and extended family. On Wednesdays, she prays specifically to St. Joseph for all those who have material or physical needs because he provided for the Holy Family.

"As I drive or shop or sweep I try to think of the intention for that day. This helps me stay focused and renewed in spirit. It also keeps me in mind of the larger Church, not just my small life and concerns," says Dorothy, who is now retired.

Dorothy says that each day she tries to pray Morning Prayer and Evening Prayer from the Liturgy of the Hours, as well as a Rosary, which she says before Blessed Sacrament at her local parish whenever possible.

"I also try to do something for someone else, be it ever so small an act of kindness," she added. "And when I get into bed, I reflect on the day, checking to see if I lived it according to God's values."

Moving Meditation

When we pray on behalf of someone else, it's called "intercessory" prayer. Think about someone you know of but don't know personally. Maybe you read a news story about a family who lost everything in a fire or a child facing a serious illness. Focus your spiritual energy on the needs of a stranger today, and see how it feels to petition God when you have nothing to gain. Throughout the day, keep coming back to that intention, exchanging your own struggles or frustrations for a prayer offered for someone who is worse off.

If you look at Dorothy's ambitious prayer "schedule," you can see the many prayer possibilities available throughout the day. In addition to the obvious prayer methods, like Morning and Evening Prayer and the Rosary, the small acts of kindness are actually a spiritual practice that brings prayer into the realm of service or charity.

Even her reflection at bedtime is a specific type of Catholic prayer known as the Examen, a careful spiritual analysis of where you may have met God during your day and where you may have rebuffed him. And woven throughout all her prayers are intercessions, those prayers uttered on behalf of others. Hers is a wonderful example of where you can go with everyday prayer if you're willing to take a little time to search out methods that work for you.

By breaking your prayers out of the usual mold, you can expand your prayer into new territory. When you open the door to everyday prayer, you change the landscape, suddenly seeing far beyond the mountains right in front of you in your own life to the oceans of needs great and small in the world all around you.

LABORS OF LOVE

The idea of turning chores into prayer may seem like a perfectly natural activity for a saint or even a former nun. But how are the rest of us Average Joes supposed to become *that* holy?

Actually, even St. Thérèse struggled with that question. At the beginning of her autobiography, she writes about her willfulness and her desire to "choose everything." It was a conscious decision and not always an easy one that her to take up regular acts of kindness and small jobs as a way of loving God more completely and deepening her prayer life in the monastery.

She recalls one particular nun who managed to "irritate" her on a regular basis. Rather than let her annoyance show, Thérèse decided that "charity" was the only way to deal with the challenge.

"So I set myself to do for this sister just what I should have done for someone I loved most dearly. Every time I met her, I prayed for her and offered God all her virtues and merits …. I tried to do as many things for her as I could, and whenever I was tempted to speak unpleasantly to her, I made myself give her a pleasant smile and tried to change the subject," she writes.

Whether the things that irritate you are chores or people or any number of issues, when you approach them with charity and prayer, you begin to transform the irritation into a blessing ... and yourself in the process.

Practical Wisdom
___

You must try continually to make all of your actions, without distinction, a sort of little conversation with God—not in a rehearsed way but just as they happen, with purity and simplicity of heart.

—Brother Lawrence, seventeenth-century French monk
___

WASHING DISHES, MAKING BEDS

I'll admit, the first time I came across the notion of linking prayer to a basic household chore, it was in a book on Buddhist spiritual practice. It caught my eye and my spiritual attention.

"I enjoy taking my time with each dish, being fully aware of the dish, the water, and each movement of my hands. I know that if I hurry in order to eat dessert sooner, the time of washing dishes will be unpleasant and not worth living. That would be a pity, for each minute, each second of life is a miracle. The dishes themselves and the fact that I am here washing them are miracles!" writes Buddhist monk Thich Nhat Hanh in *Peace Is Every Step*. "If I am incapable of washing dishes joyfully, if I want to finish them quickly so I can go and have dessert, I will be equally incapable of enjoying dessert. With the fork in my hand, I will be thinking about what to do next ...."

As I contemplated the reality of these words, I began to search for similar thought in Catholic writing and spirituality. Sure enough, it's there in different forms and throughout the centuries. For Catholics, however, the joyful action of washing a dish, mowing a lawn, or doing some other task is not occurring in a mindfulness vacuum but is instead linked by prayer to God and to others.

The medieval mystic St. Teresa of Avila once said, "God moves among the pots and pans." And Brother Lawrence, the seventeenth-century monk who wrote *Practice in the Presence of God*, said, "The time of business does not with me differ from the time of prayer; and in the noise and clatter of my kitchen, while several persons are at the same time calling for different things, I possess God in as great tranquility as if I were upon my knees at the blessed sacrament."

Notes from the Journey

Today I decided to wash my breakfast dishes by hand, rather than pile them into the dishwasher. I gently and mindfully took my bowl and spoon and favorite coffee mug and washed each piece as if I were washing a newborn baby, with care and intention and joy. When I looked up from my task, the window before me provided a clear view of sunshine glistening off a few icy patches in the backyard and, in the distance, the back porch of the new house built behind us where the woods used to be.

I resented the clear-cutting of that lot behind us. Even though the property wasn't ours, it gave us protection from the main road beyond it and from other people and created a little oasis of forest in the middle of our suburban neighborhood.

As I rinsed my dishes, I thought of the people in that new house and how happy they probably were to find such a lovely place in such a nice town. Instead of seeing only what was taken away, I saw what had been added—a home, a family, a new neighbor to greet when spring comes and we all emerge into our yards from our winter hibernation.

With my hands in the warm, sudsy water, I found a way of looking at the same old thing. And I prayed for those new neighbors, that they would find happiness in their new home.

USING YOUR PRAYER "SKILLS"

Even if you've got the best cleaning person in town, there's no getting around some basic household chores. It doesn't matter if you're a stay-at-home mom, CEO, teacher, plumber, student, or retiree, certain things simply have to be done: washing dishes, making beds, mowing lawns, wiping counters. This is the most logical place to begin adding everyday prayer into your life. Why not make the most of all that time spent doing necessary tasks? You don't need to know a special prayer; you don't need to plan ahead. You just need to be aware and use whatever prayer "skills" you have to take the next step.

Jeanne Grunert, a freelance writer, marketing consultant, and gardener extraordinaire, has found her own way to master the mindfulness of everyday tasks and stay connected to God.

"I sing with my church choir, and love to sing. I often find myself singing psalms and the Gloria while doing chores—washing dishes, scrubbing the kitchen floor, weeding. Repeating the psalms like this, lifting my heart in prayer while tackling mundane tasks, makes the task seem effortless," she told me. "This is really similar to the Eastern practice of the mantra or mantram, repeating a holy name of God or quality of God while doing mundane tasks. I sing the psalms, sometimes over and over again, as my Catholic Christian 'mantram.'"

Jeanne says that ever since she was a little girl, she's found hymns easy to memorize and sing. And because her choir regularly practices the psalms sung at Sunday Mass each week, the words to these ancient "songs" stick with her.

"God wants us to have inner peace. He wants us to quiet down enough so he can talk to us through our intuition and our hearts. We're often so busy worrying and listening to the inner 'chatter' that we can't hear him when he wants to answer us," she explains. "Singing or reciting psalms … helps still the constant inner chatter we all experience."

Think about tasks you need to do regularly that lend themselves to a certain rhythm—mowing the lawn or sweeping the floor, cleaning windows or vacuuming. Just about anything can become the backdrop for prayer when you do it with intention, mindfulness, and a heart focused on God.

Repetitive Prayer Motions

For me, raking is a chore that's so naturally suited to prayerfulness, I often seek it out on fall weekends in upstate New York where the leaf drop can be a bit overwhelming. No sooner is the job done than it needs to be done again. I think that's what makes it the perfect everyday prayer opportunity. The movement itself is rhythmic and meditative, and the very fact that the job I do will be undone with the first stiff breeze gives it a deeply philosophical bent.

We have an industrial-strength gas-powered leaf blower, but I prefer to gather the leaves the old-fashioned way. I look forward on crisp October mornings to the feel of the rake in my hands, the sound of my work boots crunching against fallen acorns, the sight of the brilliant reds and yellows and oranges all around me. It's easy to feel God's presence when I'm standing in the middle of such awesome beauty.

Sometimes I listen to spiritual music; other times I listen to the silence and the scratch, scratch, scratching of the rake against earth. I may pray actively for someone in particular or for a special intention, or I may choose to do nothing more than listen for the whisper of the Spirit and contemplate God's presence in my life.

For the record, the same can be said of snow shoveling. While my husband opts for the noisy snow blower—for which I am eternally grateful on those days when the snow is measured in feet, not inches—I choose the plastic shovel. Walking back and forth from one side of the driveway to the other, pushing the snow, lifting and heaving, breathing in air so cold it makes the inside of my nose freeze, I sense God swirling around me like the snowflakes. "I am here," he seems to say to my heart, and as I watch my neighborhood slowly go from dismal gray to sparkling white, it seems silly that I could ever doubt that.

Moving Meditation

Decide on a "chore" that lends itself to spiritual practice. It's probably best to start with something you don't absolutely dread, but if you're game, go for the worst thing on your list. Choose whatever prayer method works best for you—an Our Father for every row of lawn you mow, a decade of the Rosary as you scrub the kitchen floor, or short intercessory prayers as you change batteries in your smoke detectors. It really can be anything, anywhere. Notice if the prayer changes the way the chore feels. Do you feel less taxed and more calm? Are you thinking less of your burdens and more of other people?

THE WAITING GAME

Sometimes your best opportunities for prayer may come when you're waiting for someone or something else. So much of modern life is spent waiting—in the grocery store, at the bank, in the doctor's office, outside the kids' school, on the subway, at a red light. You can use those often-frustrating moments as doorways to prayer.

Look around a waiting room or even at the cars in a restaurant drive-thru, and you're likely to see faces glued to the glowing screens of electronic devices, fingers flying as texts are sent and status updates are posted. So often I think I have no time for prayer, but every once in a while, when I go on a technology or social networking "fast," I realize just how much time I waste scrolling around various screens looking for something, anything to occupy my thoughts.

Start looking for some of those somewhat empty moments in your life, and use the time not to surf the web but to search your soul. Turn off the screen, and turn your thoughts inward instead. You'll find that waiting takes on a whole new meaning when it's not filled with endless emails and phone calls and links.

"I once read that the number-one pastime of the saints was waiting. I often think of the saints' life stories and imagine all the action we know made them saintly happened quickly and succinctly. But in fact, many of the saints spent most of their holy lives waiting. This thought has helped shape my waiting—waiting for my children to finish a sporting practice, waiting for the egg whites to whip to a stiff peak, waiting for the bus to arrive home and safely deliver my children, waiting for the light to turn green," says Michele Bernasconi, a busy wife and mother of three daughters.

"For years now, I have chosen to fill these small waitings with Hail Marys. Mary accompanies me in my waiting and brings me to her Son. Sometimes the Hail Marys are filled with deep thought, and sometimes they're just rote. Either way, it is one way that I have woven prayer into my everyday activity," says Michele, who has become so adept at this spiritual practice she no longer needs a kitchen timer when she's cooking.

"I have four hungry mouths to feed—five if you count the dog— and so I spend a lot of my time in the kitchen. I often time the amount of time to stir, beat, knead by Hail Marys. At my pace, I pray about five Hail Marys in a minute," she told me. "If a recipe calls for 'beating at high speed for two minutes,' instead of setting the timer, I say ten Hail Marys. Works for me!"

Although Michele seems to have it all under control when it comes to everyday prayer, that wasn't always the case. She says she had a difficult time "transitioning" her prayer life from single woman with lots of time, space, and energy for contemplation to wife and mother of three children and a life of constant activity.

"It's been a challenge. I have come to realize that my actions *are* prayer and that I can work to do my activities with love, first and foremost, of God and for my loved ones," she says.

There are so many ways to weave an ongoing conversation with God into your daily life, and that's what prayer is at its core, a conversation with God. You can pray the Rosary, as Dorothy does, or sing the psalms à la Jeanne, or take a cue from Michele and say Hail Marys as you mix cake batter, or whisper prayers of petition on behalf of loved ones and strangers alike, as I try to do at times when I might otherwise be frustrated by my task.

Notes from the Journey

I recently had to spend about 90 minutes waiting for an appointment with a doctor I'd never seen before. After I'd finished filling out the necessary paperwork, there was nothing to occupy my mind but the fact that I could be headed for minor surgery.

As I felt myself beginning to worry, I looked up and saw so many other worried faces across from me and next to me. The office staff recognized most of these people as they came in, clearly signaling their familiarity with the office—and with illness.

At that moment, my worry changed to prayer, and I began to ask God to bless all these people, to give them the courage to handle the diagnosis they fear, to bring them physical healing if possible or emotional strength to get through whatever was ahead.

The prayer totally changed the dynamics of the waiting experience. What started out feeling like a waste of time became an opportunity to bring unseen graces into the life of someone else, and into my own. I tried it again when I had a second appointment that week at another office. In that case, most of the women around me were pregnant, and I found myself focusing all my spiritual energy on them and their unborn babies. I realized at that moment that I need not wait in vain ever again; there's always someone who could use my prayers.

GOING FORWARD …

† Begin to look at daily activities as a doorway to prayer. Think of chores or tasks that lend themselves to sacred rhythm.

† Follow the Little Way of St. Thérèse, learning to do small things with great love.

✝ Experiment with different types of prayer, from the Rosary to intercessory prayer to spontaneous conversation with God or total silence. Find what works for you. (If you need some guidance, check Appendix A.)

✝ Learn to see times of waiting—in a line, at the doctor, on hold—as opportunities for prayer.

4

BRINGING YOUR BODY INTO PRAYER

Although Catholic worship is somewhat physical in nature—just think of all the standing, sitting, and kneeling you do in the span of one Mass—most Catholics don't associate the physical body with spiritual growth. The practice of bringing body, mind, and spirit into alignment seems more conducive to Eastern spiritual methods, and yet as a Catholic, you can take prayer to a whole new level—and a host of new locations—if you're willing to see physical exercise as a pathway to transcendence, or at least inner stillness.

For too long now, there has been a disconnect between body and spirit in Catholic prayer practices, with some people even viewing the body as the enemy of spiritual progress. But that mind-body dualism wasn't always the case, and it's certainly out of place when you get down to the heart of the Catholic faith.

After all, our God *became* human, taking on a body just like ours to save us, coming into the world through a woman. At the Last Supper, he gave us his Body and Blood as spiritual food. After suffering a brutal death on the cross, he rose from the dead—not in a metaphorical way but in an actual bodily way. Our God ascended into heaven, body and soul; his body was not left behind as some castoff unworthy of eternal life. And our faith teaches that we, too, will rise, body and soul, on the last day.

Surely our humanity can't be such a detriment to prayer if God saw fit to place the body so squarely at the center of salvation.

TWO HALVES OF THE SAME WHOLE

"How should we go to God in prayer? In and through our bodies, the way God came to us." I felt a ripple of joy as I absorbed those words of Paulist Father Thomas Ryan during a workshop called "Pray All Ways" at Kripalu Center for Yoga and Health in Lenox, Massachusetts. As I sat cross-legged on the floor with 25 other retreat participants, I smiled upon hearing aloud what I always knew in my heart: prayer can and should be a physical as well as a spiritual experience.

Rest, good food, friendship, and exercise are all part of spirituality in a "seamless unity," Father Tom explained, pointing out that you can easily find those things in the Gospel stories.

Jesus can often be found sitting down to a meal with friends, strangers, and sinners alike. You can also find many other "physical" elements to Jesus' deeply spiritual teachings throughout Scripture: the "man born blind," whose sight is restored when Jesus makes a mixture of dirt and spit and rubs it on the man's eyes; the woman who washes Jesus' feet with her tears and dries them with her hair; the countless people who follow after Jesus, begging him to heal them with nothing more than a touch; and Jesus himself bending down to wash the feet of his disciples before the Last Supper.

As Jesus enters into his Passion, the physical reality of God Incarnate is exposed in the most powerful and brutal ways. He sweats blood as he prays in the Garden of Gethsemane, asking his Father to take the cup of suffering from him if it is his will. Not long after, Jesus is betrayed by Judas with a kiss. Beatings, scourging, and a crown of thorns leave the body of Christ battered but not broken. Finally, he is nailed to a cross and raised up to die a very public and painful physical death.

One of my favorite scenes from the movie *Jesus of Nazareth* is when Jesus' body is taken down from the cross and laid on the muddy ground in the afternoon rain. His mother comes over and wails in anguish, cradling the limp body of her beloved son in a scene reminiscent of Michelangelo's *Pieta*. The human suffering and grief before, during, and after the Crucifixion is the ultimate example of the physical elements that are deeply embedded in salvation history.

This is not a faith that's pristine and devoid of the messiness of humanity, but one that literally gets down in the dirt and demonstrates that transcendence can come through all the things that make you human, not in spite of them.

BODY IN MOTION, SPIRIT IN STILLNESS

Father Tom, the Paulist priest I mentioned earlier in this chapter, is a trained yoga teacher who blends the ancient Hindu practice with Catholicism. For him, the body-spirit connection is central to Catholic prayer practice.

"Westerners have been conditioned to think that prayer is mostly a mental activity, largely associated with the brain. But prayer is not a bodiless experience done only in the head, nor only in the heart. It is an experience of the whole person," he writes in *Reclaiming the Body in Christian Spirituality*. "When we pray, we should do so as a whole person and with those gestures and postures that seem most natural to us and are most meaningful to us."

So rather than see your body as something you have to ignore or get around in order to move forward spiritually, you can begin to look for ways to bring the two together, discovering in the process a multitude of opportunities to pray in the everyday while going about your physical activities.

If the idea of using your body to pray seems a bit foreign or makes you uncomfortable, stop for a moment to think about the physical actions that are so much a part of your Catholic faith you may not even notice them. You probably make the Sign of the Cross every time you enter a church or start a prayer. You're likely to genuflect or bow before the altar, kneel during the consecration, sing with the choir, maybe even clap, depending on how "contemporary" your parish's music program is. If you've ever been to an ordination, you've seen the men preparing for the priesthood or diaconate lying prostrate before the altar. All these postures and movements are physical reminders of what we are attempting to achieve through prayer: humility before and union with God.

To move to the next level, you simply need to start looking at everyday movements that lend themselves to prayer and praise, contemplation and conversation. Even if you're not a gym rat and don't have an exercise "routine," you can find plenty of opportunities in the space of a normal day to use even small physical actions as points of prayer.

Practical Wisdom

Do you not know that your body is a temple of the Holy Spirit within you, whom you have from God, and that you are not your own? For you have been purchased at a price. Therefore glorify God in your body.

—1 Corinthians 6:20

When I took my first yoga class more than 20 years ago, I was in a bit of a crisis in terms of the Catholic faith of my birth. My mother had recently died, and I had moved out of my family home for the first time and across the country. I was searching in so many ways and came upon yoga through a friend who knew a teacher who held classes in her home. There, on a mat in an empty living room, I learned how to stretch and settle my body in new ways, ways that allowed me to more easily enter a spiritual realm that has always beckoned to me.

I tend to be a body in constant motion, moving from work to exercise to gardening to volunteer activities and more without any downtime in between. Quieting myself for prayer does not come naturally to me. My mind wants to work on all the things that need to be done. My body wants to twitch and itch and fold and unfold, never content to just be still in one place.

Yoga, however, showed me that I could actually use physical activity to slow myself down and create a place of stillness within, even as I did a sun salutation. Suddenly, my penchant for movement was actually a help, not a hindrance, when it came to my spiritual life. At a time of personal confusion and chaos, yoga gave me a peaceful place to reconnect with God, a way to listen to what he had to say above the din of my life, and an open door that led back to the richness of my own Catholic faith.

Whether you opt for yoga or running, walking or cycling, dancing or skiing, whatever your physical activity of choice, it, too, can become your entry point to interior stillness. You would think the two would be diametrically opposed—movement and stillness—and yet the one can create an environment that brings the body into closer harmony with the spirit, leaving you with a peaceful "eye" in the midst of your everyday storms, a balanced and quiet core even as your body moves along the pavement or across a dance floor.

Moving Meditation

What's your favorite physical activity? Have you ever attempted to weave prayer or even silent reflection into your routine? Experiment with one exercise or activity that comes naturally to you—jogging, walking, biking, weightlifting, etc. Put away your ear buds or whatever other audio-visual distractions usually keep your mind otherwise occupied, and try saying a favorite prayer or simply listening to the silence or the noises around you. Notice how your mind and heart respond.

EXERCISE AS A PATH TO SPIRITUAL GROWTH

I don't know about you, but I'm typically one of those people who needs to have Guns N' Roses' "Welcome to the Jungle" or something equally loud and intense pounding through my headphones if I'm going to have a successful run. On those rare occasions when I find myself on the elliptical machine at the Y or on my neighborhood jogging path with a dead battery in my iPod, my initial reaction is to turn around and go home. I know I won't have nearly the drive or stamina without music to keep me going.

Praying during a run is simply not optimal for me, at least not in terms of calories burned or miles covered. It was a stretch, then, when I decided to venture out one afternoon without my music mix. So many friends had told me how their daily runs were augmented by prayer, specifically the Rosary, and how their prayer was, in turn, augmented by exercise. I figured I'd give it a shot and see what I was missing.

I started running, and all I could hear was the pounding of my feet and the sound of my breathing—labored before I even had time to work up a sweat. I tried saying a Hail Mary, but it felt flat and some-what forced. I jogged a few more blocks, berating myself mentally for being unable to pull this off. Then I decided to drop the formal prayers, and I just started praying for all those people I knew who were sick or going through a rough time. Before I knew it, a half-mile was behind me. Next, I moved onto my children, husband, extended family, and friends. Another half-mile done.

By the time I was more than halfway through my run, I realized I was less tired than normal and more focused. I was so aware of the sounds of the neighborhood, from chirping birds to grinding gar-bage trucks. Even the leaves and clouds seemed crisper against the blue autumn sky, and everything felt tangibly connected to God. It was a totally different experience for me, one that really opened my eyes to what is possible, what I am capable of, when I'm willing to step out of my comfort zone and embrace something new in my prayer life.

Traditional exercise is often the perfect complement to traditional prayer. The repetitive movement lends itself to meditation in mo-tion. Putting one foot in front of the other, pedaling up a steep hill, skiing down a snow-covered mountain, even doing the weight cir-cuit at the gym can provide you with a rhythm just right for prayer, the words moving with your body and your breath.

RACING TOWARD HEAVEN

Sister Madonna Buder, known as the "Iron Nun," was 48 years old when her spiritual director suggested she give running a try. That was back in 1978. Since then, the Sister of the Good Shepherd and champion triathlete has completed more than three dozen marathons and 340 triathlons—and she's still going strong at 81 years old, proving that prayer and physical fitness are perfect partners.

Only a week after taking up running for the first time, Sister Madonna signed up for an 8.2-mile race, which she planned to run in honor of her brother, who at the time was struggling with personal issues. In a pair of donated $12.99 sneakers, the nun set out to change the course of her brother's life and her own through exercise and prayer.

"All I knew at the time was that I was running on faith, and I prayed while I ran. Afterward, I realized it was a different kind of prayer posture. Besides using my heart and head, when I ran my whole body was involved in the petitioning," Sister Madonna writes in her book, *The Grace to Race*. "I had no idea what effect my running prayers might eventually have on my brother's life, but somehow I knew I was being transformed by it myself."

You might not be able to lace up a pair of cheap sneakers and make history, but you can go for a walk or jog around the block or your favorite park, or sign up for a local fun run with the intention of dedicating it to someone who needs your prayers. Even a run on the treadmill in your basement can be an opportunity for spiritual connection if you open yourself, as Sister Madonna did, to the possibilities available to you right where you are. She started with a pair of borrowed sneakers on a beach. You might start on the track at your local high school or on a hike-and-bike trail in your town. You don't have to be a champion; you just have to be willing.

Peggy Bowes, author of *The Rosary Workout*, frequently prayed during exercise, but one day, when she went out to do some "interval training"—short periods of intense exercise followed by low-intensity "recovery" exercise—she discovered a new way to incorporate the Rosary into a more structured routine.

"I ran faster during the prayers that separate the decades—Glory Be, Fatima prayer, mystery announcement and Our Father—and recovered during the ten Hail Marys. I found that this actually aided my meditation because it emphasized the transition between mysteries," she told me. "I often find that my deepest and most fruitful meditation occurs during exercise."

Peggy relied on her experience as a personal trainer and metabolic testing specialist to create a structured program that uses the Rosary to help runners and other cardio-fitness junkies become more physically fit while they grow spiritually. She says the key lies in using rhythmic exercise to "clear the mind," which allows people to enter more easily into a Rosary meditation even as they do high-intensity workouts. The Rosary Workout uses a gentle progression to help move users through nine levels. Whether you're new to running or new to the Rosary, Bowes provides the background needed to become adept at both.

In her own life, Bowes has seen the power of her prayer on the go. It comes to her automatically as she laces up her sneakers now. And to keep it from becoming monotonous, she has found creative ways to change it up.

"Since I pray so many Rosaries, I can pray for a variety of intentions, not just those affecting my family or me. I'll offer my Rosary for the homeless man I gave some cash to or the couple who always sits behind me at daily Mass," she says. "It helps me to practice humility and charity by praying for others who will never know I did so."

For Emily Szelest, a 20-something church youth minister in upstate New York, even the rigors of lacrosse didn't keep her from weaving prayer into play. She was goalkeeper for the University of Pennsylvania, Division 1 women's lacrosse team, so workouts were pretty intense—running three times a week, lifting the same amount, plus a normal practice and game schedule.

"A lot of times when we were doing the workouts or had to be out in the cold for a while, I would imagine what it must have been like for Jesus—either the Holy Family traveling in the cold, or Christ personified in an individual who is homeless and must endure staying outside for long periods of time in the cold," she told me. She also noted that when she would have to do difficult runs or lifts and didn't think she could go any further, she would imagine Jesus carrying his cross on the road to Calvary.

"There were always ways to use the pain of the moment of exercise, or joy of relief and accomplishment, and transform it into some kind of meditation on Christ's life, or how Christ's life is lived today through each person struggling or experiencing joy in some way," Emily explains.

Practical Wisdom

The gift of God is not separated from our nature, nor is it far from those who look for it. It dwells within every one of us, ignored and forgotten, choked with the cares and pleasures of life, but it is rediscovered when we turn our minds to it.

—St. Gregory of Nyssa, fourth century

MEDITATIVE WALKS

Maybe you don't have the need for speed or heart-pounding cardio routines. Maybe slow and steady is more up your alley. That's just fine. In fact, that's the perfect pace for a truly meditative walk, something that has no particular goal other than entering into the moment and steeping every step in prayer.

You can find meditative walking in many prayer traditions, often accompanied by physical markers or paths—like a labyrinth—that allow you to lose yourself in prayer without losing yourself on a busy city street or in a deserted wood. It's important that a true meditative walk be done in a safe place where getting caught up in your prayers or your thoughts won't put you at risk of getting hit by a car.

Reverend Robin Craig, pastor of Nankin Federated Church in Nankin, Ohio, says that walking the labyrinth has been part of her Christian prayer practice for a long time, probably dating to her experience with the "grandmother of labyrinths" in the Chartres Cathedral in France.

"The rhythmic repetition of a labyrinth walk is appealing to me. Sometimes I walk a labyrinth praying for various people, changing names at each turn. Sometimes I do the same thing with Scripture or a book of prayers or essays: a new verse or sentence upon which to meditate with every turn," she told me, adding that the labyrinth at the Jesuit Retreat Center at Guelph, Ontario, remains her favorite labyrinth walk.

"I spend a huge amount of my prayer time walking, or a huge amount of my walking time in prayer," she explains, noting that even when she's not in a labyrinth, her walking mimics that style— slow and meditative. "I never thought of those walks as related to the labyrinth, but I suppose the idea is the same. I often use city blocks and intersections to structure my prayer: again, focusing on a name or a line in an essay or poem for each block. As with the turns in the labyrinth, if I reach an intersection in the street and I've gone off track in my mind, the recognition of where I am physically pulls me back into prayer."

The practice of walking a labyrinth has made a serious comeback in recent years, with spiritual seekers of all denominations giving this ancient tradition a try. Within a 50-mile radius of my home in upstate New York, I can drive in almost any direction and find a labyrinth, from the small, grassy version at the Kripalu center, to an indoor stone version in a busy suburban Catholic parish, to a canvas labyrinth at a nearby community center, to a portable "virtual" pewter version that comes with a tiny stylus. On a women's retreat, I once "walked" a small paper labyrinth, using my finger to slowly move down the path, which looks like a maze but really isn't a maze since you can't get lost or make a wrong turn.

Some traditional Catholics have issues with the labyrinth, saying it's too closely related to pagan tradition, but just as many emphasize the dramatic way the labyrinth walk will slow down even the most fidgety pray-ers and encourage them to shift their focus from achieving a certain goal to reveling in the journey itself.

If you can't find a labyrinth or if that's just not your style, you can give meditative walking a try in any location that allows you to move slowly and in safety—a quiet side street, a local nature preserve, a botanical garden, or even a local mall during the "off" hours of early morning. Granted, it won't be exactly the same as a grand labyrinth in a cathedral, but you may just find that it's even better, a true experience of slow prayer within the rush of life.

HIKING AND CAMPING

Somewhere between triathlon and labyrinth is a happy medium that probably suits just about anyone. Walking, hiking, and even camping can be opportunities for spiritual reflection and prayer, a beautiful coupling of physical activity and natural beauty.

Whether you live in a city, suburb, or rural outpost, you most likely have some favorite outdoor haunts, places where you can be alone in a crowd or just plain alone. Even if you don't have any parks or trails near your home, you've likely got a few treasured escapes that give you space and time to breathe when life gets to be overwhelming. Any of those places are wonderful spots for bringing prayer into movement.

Salesian Father Michael Mendl is a regular hiker and camper. Although he doesn't pray "explicitly" when walking on busy city streets or even in the woods—both demand a certain amount of attention to remain safe, he reminds—he often finds that the Spirit moves him to prayer in the most unexpected ways and places.

"Many years ago I was biking in a run-down section of Columbus, Ohio, and saw some homes being renovated. For whatever reason (God knows), they became an instant image for me of what the Lord will do for us in the resurrection, transforming our worn-out, beat-up, corrupted bodies. So in either the city or the woods something may trigger an instant meditation if we're open to the Holy Spirit. Obviously you can't plan a moment of the Spirit's inspiration," he told me.

Father Mike says that if you offer your whole self to God and your whole day to God, which anyone can do regardless of physical abilities or schedules, then any time you give your full attention to what you're doing, you're turning it into prayer.

"That is one of the teachings of the spiritual masters. In the novitiate they tried to instill in us the principle '*Age quod agis*,' literally, 'Do what you are doing,'" explains Father Mike, recalling the years of education and training all religious sisters, brothers, and priests go through before taking their vows. "In other words, concentrate on the task at hand and do it well."

Camping is another matter. In that case, Father Mike does explicitly pray, bringing along his "breviary" (the prayer book containing the readings, hymns, prayers, and psalms of the Liturgy of the Hours) and a Mass kit so he can pray the Hours and celebrate Mass even in the most remote locations.

"A lay person can't bring Mass on the trail of course, but you can always bring a bit of the Liturgy of the Hours or some little collection of favorite prayers or just the Rosary," he said, adding that prayer is often more difficult at home where there are so many distractions than when he's out at a campsite or on a hike. "After some hours of hiking, it feels good to sit down quietly. To sit with the Lord or his mother is a good way to spend a few minutes before either resuming the trail or getting about camp duties like finding firewood or cooking."

DANCE, YOGA, AND MORE

You don't have to participate in one of the more typical exercise
outlets to make the prayer-body connection work for you. Maybe
ballet has always been your thing, or perhaps you've found your
physical home in t'ai chi, yoga, belly dancing, or any number of
more creative physical activities. Or maybe you opt for skiing,
horseback riding, or sailing. Every single one of those options, plus
countless others, lend themselves to prayer, perhaps even more so
than traditional exercise because they often involve serene studios
or majestic natural settings, things that typically inspire spiritual
pursuits.

Colleen Smith, author and founder of Friday Jones Publishing in
Denver, Colorado, says she is just as likely to fall into everyday
prayer on the ski slopes as in her garden or in a yoga studio, although sometimes downhill prayer can be more of a challenge.

"Initially, I prayed for my own protection because alpine skiing
includes risk. I have a devotion to St. Bernard of Montjoux, patron
and protector of skiers. I send up a prayer to him every day before
I ski and at the end of every ski day. I pray for safety—not only
for myself, but for everybody on the mountain or any mountain,"
Colleen told me, saying she has been known to "pray in despera-
tion" when skiing in a blinding blizzard.

"Since ancient times, many cultures associated the mountains with
divinity …. The mountains stimulate mysticism. Being on top of the
world is breathtaking and transcendent. The vistas inspire awe. Up
there, I get the big picture. I forget about all my other worries and
focus on my turns. I'm present when I'm skiing because the sport
requires presence for safety," she explains.

It's not just the majesty of creation that makes skiing prayerful for
Smith. It's the fact that her sport makes her appreciate the physical
abilities and financial blessings that allow her to pursue skiing. It's
the childlike joy that rises to the surface and restores her when she's
on the slopes.

"Recreation figures into my recipe for being a healthy, happy human being. My experience is that when I'm more in touch with my body and my breath, I'm more in touch with my spirit," Colleen says. "When we bring our bodies into prayer, worship can take on a kinetic element that to me feels like a prayer of rejoicing, but also a prayer of action: faith finding form in deeds. It takes faith to step onto a yoga mat or off a mountaintop."

I experienced that leap of faith when I was on retreat at Kripalu. Father Tom invited us to participate in a sunrise yoga session that would be set to Scripture rather than Sanskrit chant. I showed up with my mat, sleep-deprived but excited for this new experience. As we moved from chair pose to mountain pose to the words of Psalm 139—"You know when I sit and when I stand"—it occurred to me, perhaps for the first time, that I could set my yoga routine to something other than New Age music.

As with the labyrinth, some Catholics are leery of or downright opposed to yoga as part of a Catholic prayer practice, but for others (present company included) it is a viable option, providing a graceful and grace-filled way to bring the physical and spiritual together, no matter your particular faith tradition.

What works for you may not work for someone else. The key to weaving prayer into exercise is to find an activity you love so much you won't get tired of it or consider it a chore. If you don't like to run, try biking or swimming or dancing. Don't jump into a new or unappealing activity and try to weave prayer into it right off the bat. It won't work, and you're likely to get discouraged.

Find your bliss, as the pop sentiment goes. Seek out the exercise or activity that speaks to you—body, mind, and spirit. Then infuse it with prayer, whatever prayer works for you. Bring together elements you love so the experience as a whole becomes far greater than the sum of its parts.

In Sickness and in Health

Not everyone can swoosh down a ski slope or run a marathon or even hike a nature trail. Some people have chronic or permanent health conditions that prevent strenuous or regular exercise. Even if you're perfectly fit right now, there's a good chance that at one time or another, you've struggled with an illness or injury. None of us can avoid at least occasional pain and suffering, even if we faithfully take our vitamins and cut back on red meat.

Part of the theme of gratitude that's meant to be an undercurrent in our prayer life involves finding a way to accept and be grateful for your body, even with its clicking joints and aching muscles, even with digestive issues that slow you down or the hip problem that keeps you from walking around the block. As much as prayer can be part of your physical exercise routine, it can also be part of your physical issues and your physical healing. Some might say prayer is even more critical when you're battling ailments that not only atrophy your actual muscles but your emotional and spiritual strength as well.

I recently had to deal with a minor injury and condition that totally threw me off course. All my regular exercise routines were forbidden in an effort to heal torn tissue. I was given a set of exercises that focused on the tiniest internal movements and lots of deep and controlled breathing. It was like torture for me. I wanted the big, grand, muscle-building movements of my previous exercise plan; this new path seemed downright pathetic.

And so I grumbled and withheld, doing the exercises now and then as opposed to every day, maybe even twice each day, to get me to where I needed to be. Although I was only hurting myself, I acted like a petulant child, refusing to play if I couldn't do so according to my rules.

The interesting thing is that this little temper tantrum of mine really affected my prayer life, even though it started as a purely physical issue. As my exercise routine went by the wayside, the spiritual darkness deepened. Anger and self-pity started to fill the space where acceptance and determination had once been. I started to glare at God. Eventually, I gave God the silent treatment, but I was the only one feeling the emptiness and isolation.

Then I realized that perhaps I was meant to learn something from this experience. Maybe my inability to settle into the small, quiet movements I was required to do was a sign that I was exactly where I needed to be. Maybe slowing down was the prescription for a life lived at full tilt, and a minor injury was the only thing that was going to stop me in my tracks. I slowly started to open up to the idea that this bout of physical discomfort and discouragement was just another part of my path. I could go willingly or fight the whole way. I chose the former.

Of course, I had it easy. My problem was minor. Plenty of other people have true suffering—physical, emotional, and spiritual. Prayer can bring real comfort in those difficult moments.

Finding Meaning in Suffering

I have a friend who has been terminally ill for quite some time. She originally hoped to live long enough to know her twin grandchildren had been born. After she passed that milestone, she set her sights on getting to her beloved Cape Cod with her husband one last time and then on meeting those twin grandchildren when they and their parents made the cross-country trip for a visit. She has outlived all her "bucket list" goals, fighting her years-long battle against ovarian cancer from her living room couch with the help of her husband and a team from hospice.

Every once in a while, I'll stop in to see Maureen, although now the visits are limited to two or three minutes at most since she is so tired and so weak. Yet despite her weakness, she is a powerful prayer warrior and a great inspiration. She rarely talks about herself, asking instead, "How are the two people I'm praying for?" referring to friends I've asked her to include in her daily prayers. I consider

Maureen's prayers especially powerful, coming as they do from a place of deep suffering, total surrender, and unwavering faith.

Sometimes people talk about finding meaning in a terminal illness or strength in suffering, and it can be hard for those of us on the outside to understand how it could be so. But there it is, a truth that seems almost universal among people of faith: suffering can be a pathway to a deeper relationship with God and with others, if you're willing to look for lessons amid the sorrow and strife.

In her moving book, *I Will Not Die an Unlived Life*, author Dawna Markova writes about her battle with cancer and what it taught her about herself: "Crisis can force us deep enough to find out who we really are and what we truly love, and it is here, where there are no masks, no one else's values or beliefs, that passion lives. ... Loss can remind us that, as human beings, we struggle with doubt and darkness in an imperfect world where suffering and grace both abound."

Sometimes prayer isn't easy if you or someone you love is suffering. You may be angry at God—so angry you're not on speaking terms. That's okay. God can take it. Just try to keep coming back to that place of prayer, as you sit in a doctor's office, wait with a loved one for a treatment, or walk the halls of a hospital.

A life of prayer does not equal a life without suffering, but if you've developed a regular prayer life, your relationship with God will see you through the roughest storms—even when you don't understand God's plan.

SELF-CARE AS DOORWAY TO PRAYER

Too often, the whole body-spirit divide among Catholics has led to outright disdain for the body. The body has been seen not only as a stumbling block to spiritual growth but as something deserving only minimal attention, maybe even a little abuse via neglect, lest you become narcissistic or too focused on physical pleasure. For a long time, there was a sense that wanting to wear nice clothes, go to a spa, pay for a gym membership, or paint your toenails red were signs of vanity, which was, of course, only a skip and a jump away from lust, one of the deadliest deadly sins.

So many Catholics fell into the mistaken belief that caring for their bodies in a loving and generous way, even liking their bodies at all, was tantamount to sin. In recent years, we've reversed that a bit, although that's more a secular endeavor than a Catholic one. We need to reclaim that understanding that our bodies are temples and deserve to be treated as such.

If you want some cold, hard proof that even the Church universal understands this reality, here's a passage from the 1965 Vatican II document *Gadium et Spes,* the Pastoral Constitution of the Church in the Modern World:

> Though made of body and soul, man is one.
> Through his bodily composition he gathers to
> himself the elements of the material world; thus
> they reach their crown through him, and through
> him raise their voice in free praise of the Creator.
> For this reason man is not allowed to despise his
> bodily life, rather he is obliged to regard his body
> as good and honorable since God has created it
> and will raise it up on the last day.

Obviously, when I talk about caring for your body from a Catholic perspective, I'm not talking about spending outrageous amounts of money on jewels and fur coats. I'm looking at this from a more organic approach: healthy foods to nourish your body, nice clothes to make you look your best, medical care when you're sick, massage for your sore muscles—whatever it takes to make you look and feel like the much-loved child of God you are.

The best thing you can do for your body costs no money at all: develop an attitude of generosity, acceptance, and love toward your-self. Far too many people are caught in an "I'm-no-good" frame of mind, which only drags down your spiritual life. God did not create you to wallow in self-hatred but to accept his love and return it to others and the world around you. But that can be a hard message to take to heart.

I was recently cleaning out the cabinet under my bathroom sink when I had a minor revelation. As I unloaded various jars and bottles—many of them unopened—I came face to face with the fact that I have an incredibly hard time allowing myself to be pampered. Luxury seems extravagant at best, and vain at worst. I was amazed at how many shower gels, body lotions, and scented soaps were gathering dust because I was saving them for a day, an event, a year I could deem special enough.

If you've ever felt that way, I challenge you to crack open a bottle or box of whatever it is you hoard because you're "not good enough"— bubble bath, red wine, shade-grown coffee, perfume—and give yourself the gift of self-care, with a prayer of gratitude thrown in.

By approaching self-care from a place of spiritual awareness, you can bring a whole new dimension to your daily rituals, from washing your hair and bathing to making that long overdue appointment with a nutritionist. The danger of vanity is balanced by the focus on your body as a gift from God. This is not about how good *you* are but about how great *he* is.

Moving Meditation

When you begin your morning ritual tomorrow, do so from a place of loving kindness. Approach everything from a place of mindfulness. As you brush your teeth, comb your hair, and get dressed, give thanks to God for the creation that is you. Let the rituals of your routine become your new prayer positions. Do you carry around heavy emotional burdens just beneath the surface, beliefs about yourself that keep you from loving as you should? Let go of those mistaken beliefs, and reclaim your connection to your body and the life God has given you.

Going Forward ...

✝ The body is not the enemy to spiritual progress. You can use your body—through exercise and other physical activities—to further your prayer life.

✝ Physical movement, when done mindfully and prayerfully, can lead to interior stillness.

✝ Whatever your favorite activity, from jogging and hiking to yoga and dance, you can make prayer part of its natural rhythm.

✝ Times of illness, injury, and suffering can provide difficult but powerful insights along your spiritual journey.

✝ Caring for your body is not self-indulgent but completely in keeping with the scriptural understanding of your body as a temple of the Holy Spirit. Begin to see yourself with the eyes of love.

5

THE WORK OF
YOUR HANDS

Most people have at least one hobby, talent, skill, or interest that stands out as their favorite way to spend free time. Whether it's cooking or gardening, knitting or blacksmithing, painting a canvas or painting a room, the activities you love most are perfect conduits for prayer. Why not bring a new level of devotion to a favorite pastime?

This method of praying in the everyday is probably the easiest of all the daily prayer options. Unlike household chores or even exercise, where you may start off in a negative or neutral place, favorite activities are likely to inspire joy, peace, and quiet introspection even before you layer prayer on top. These are the activities that make you feel at one with the world, the things that bring out the very best in you, so adding prayer to their routine and rhythm comes naturally.

FINDING GOD IN THE KITCHEN

If spending time at your kitchen counter preparing delicious dinners and decadent desserts is your idea of relaxation and fun, you're in luck. Chopping, cooking, and even eating are optimal prayer times. When you start to look at the individual actions that make up your food prep experience, you'll see that they're ready-made for spirituality.

Spiritual Sautéing and Simmering

I cook for a group of somewhat picky eaters. Two out of our five are vegetarians (including yours truly), so we're typically trying to come up with dinners that please everyone on the food spectrum, from the devoted carnivores to the tween vegetarian who doesn't really like vegetables all that much. It's a challenge to say the least. But I love to cook, and so most of the time I'm pretty happy to settle down at my cutting board with a pile of fresh vegetables, salad, fruit, tofu, and more while the world spins wildly around me.

There's something satisfying about rhythmically chopping onions, carrots, and celery while I look out the window at the trees just starting to bud. If I stay in the present moment, if I'm able to maintain a mindful attitude, I can enter into a meditative experience despite the noise and chaos just over my shoulder.

Making something from "nothing" has a sense of the sacred about it as well. What were once just a few simple vegetables in the refrigerator bin become, with a little love and attention, a steaming pot of soup bubbling on the stove or a colorful pasta primavera sitting at the center of the dinner table.

Practical Wisdom

Ordinariness is the path. God lies close at hand.

—Esther de Waal, contemporary spiritual writer

Sometimes the most profound cooking experiences are those that are the most basic—making dough, washing greens, sautéing vegetables, whipping cream. Kneading flour and water into a soft, elastic mound of yeasty goodness or swishing romaine lettuce around in a cold water bath—these are actions that call us back to something essential, providing a lovely slice of time and space for the inclusion of prayer.

You don't have to be a gourmet to experience these powerful prayer moments while cooking. Simply begin to notice the ingredients you're using, the way you're approaching them and cooking them, and the way you're serving them. If you do everything with attention and *intention*, you can turn a seemingly unimpressive meal into a moment of pure joy.

Begin to use the otherwise mundane moments of cooking as entry points for prayer. Pray Hail Marys, as Michele told us in Chapter 3, as you beat cake batter. Pray for the intentions of those you know who are ill or suffering as you scrub or chop vegetables. Add blessings along with ingredients as you stir together your meal.

Many faith traditions emphasize the importance of cooking from a place of love and peace rather than a place of anger or frustration. Some go as far to say food tastes better when cooked in a mindful and prayerful way. Does it? I can't guarantee it does, but I can guarantee it won't hurt to try, and you're likely to have a much happier and centered attitude if you approach cooking from a place of prayer. When you chop or when you stir, be in the moment without trying to escape to another place in your mind. In that moment, look for God amid the pots and pans, amid the peeled carrots and baking potatoes, even amid the mess your cooking makes all around you.

CREATING MEALTIME RITUALS

One way to foster a more spiritual attitude in the kitchen and around the table is to create little rituals that ground your actions in the sacred. Set your table with love, and add a special element. You'd be surprised what a single candle can do to quell the typical chaos around our family dinner table, for example. Whether you live alone, with your spouse, or with a whole gang of kids, you can bring a prayerful attitude to meals through simple and time-tested rituals.

Grace before meals is the most obvious place to start. At our house, grace is often said while at least one person is chewing. Even so, we plow ahead, knowing that those few simple words uttered before we eat remind us of our blessings, reconnect us to God, and create a little pause in our otherwise full lives.

I recently took my tween daughter, Olivia, with me for a weekend speaking engagement in a neighboring state. As we sat in the hotel restaurant on a Friday night during Lent, trying to find something that didn't contain meat and wasn't deep-fried to boot, I was a little less than centered. My mind was on the talk I had to give the next day, on the possibility that maybe I should have driven to a nicer restaurant, on the smell of stale smoke emanating from the man seated at the table right behind me.

As we were about to dig into our appetizer of mozzarella sticks (so much for nothing deep-fried), Olivia stopped me and said, "Wait, we didn't say grace." And so we stopped, and we bowed our heads there in the busy restaurant, made the Sign of the Cross, and connected across our gooey cheese and marinara sauce. I felt humbled by my daughter's ability to keep certain things at the fore, even in less-than-perfect circumstances, and I felt happy that our at-home practice has sunk deep into her bones and will likely stay with her forever, even if it ebbs and flows over the course of her life.

You can try different things to bring mindfulness and prayer to your meals. Try eating a meal in total silence—a real challenge in our always-connected, never-quiet world. If quiet doesn't suit you, put on some Gregorian chant or other soothing spiritual music.

I'm a fan of Pandora, the online site that allows you to create "stations" with certain types of music or artists. I have stations for chant, "yoga music," meditation, Christian pop, old church standards, and even a Hildegard of Bingen station in honor of the medieval mystic and composer. Whatever mood I'm in—at my desk, in my kitchen, on my yoga mat, or in my prayer chair—if I don't want silence, I've got a great prayerful alternative.

If you often eat alone, make a point to experience a silent meal on the deepest level. Silence phones, and close laptops. Turn off music and television. Put away magazines and sales flyers, and eat slowly in total stillness. It will give you new appreciation for the food on your plate, the atmosphere in your dining space, and the silence available if only you make the space for it. Complete silence can be extremely loud in its own stripped-down way. When coupled with a mindful meal, it will transport you to a whole new spiritual zone.

Moving Meditation

The first time you attempt to eat a meal in total silence, your body and mind will rebel. Your thoughts will race, and you'll be tempted to rush through the meal. Try this exercise to force yourself into a place of mindfulness: eat your entire meal with your eating utensil in your nondominant hand. You'll be surprised how difficult it is to go from righty to lefty (or vice versa). It will require all of your attention, which is exactly what you want. Use the slowness forced on you by this practice to enter into a meditative meal.

SEASONAL CELEBRATIONS

When it comes to bringing prayer into the kitchen, Catholic tradition has an abundance of seasonal offerings to support your efforts. So many holidays and holy days are connected to food-related celebrations or spiritual themes, it's easy to come up with a rotation of practices that can anchor your mealtime prayers.

Advent, the four-week preparation for Christmas that also marks the start of the Church year, is a wonderful time to weave the symbols and traditions of faith into home life. We always put an Advent wreath in the center of our kitchen table, and each night before we eat dinner, we light the appropriate candles and say our blessing. Sometimes we include short Scripture readings or other seasonal prayers to make our nightly ritual a little different and extra special.

During Lent, the 40 days leading up to Easter, our before-meal ritual takes a different tone. Instead of a festive wreath, we put a simple cardboard "rice bowl" in the center of our table. Sponsored by Catholic Relief Services, an international aid organization, the rice bowl and its accompanying calendar and printed material reminds us there are so many hungry people in the world who need our help. Through our Lenten sacrifices, we collect some change or dollars and add them to the rice bowl week by week. We send what we've collected to Catholic Relief Services when Lent is over. Sometimes I add a simple wooden cross to our Lenten "tablescape," and we pray for people we know who are sick or in need of some extra prayers.

Although Advent and Lent are the most obvious seasonal celebrations, you can find plenty of other ways to bring Catholic traditions into your kitchen, utilizing ethnic traditions from the many cultures that make our Church truly Catholic. Make St. Lucy bread on the feast of St. Lucy (December 13), King Cake for Mardi Gras (Fat Tuesday), or pretzels on Lenten days of fasting. (Check Appendix C for resources on seasonal celebrations.)

Of course, the centerpiece of this food-faith connection is Eucharist, the spiritual food that lies at the heart of Catholic belief and at the center of the Mass, which is really a feast shared among spiritual family members. It's not surprising that mealtime would be the perfect time for prayer at home. After all, mealtime is *the* time for prayer as a Catholic community.

"We refer to receiving the Eucharist as Holy Communion. It's all about communion; it's all about family. It really should be the same around our kitchen table," says Jeff Young, a writer and blogger known as the Catholic Foodie.

"Families are so fragmented today, with no time to cook, with multiple family members in different parts of town at dinnertime just about every night of the week. It is nearly impossible to get everyone together to simply share a meal," he told me. "And sadly, in many families—like my own growing up—even when all the members are together, meals cannot genuinely be shared with lively conversation and growing relationships because those conversations are drowned out by the TV or radio that's on in the background. Talk about fragmentation. Everyone is there seated at the table and there's no real communion going on."

To create a sense of communion at home, Jeff recommends establishing some rituals in addition to saying grace before meals and celebrating the liturgical seasons. The rituals don't have to be inherently spiritual but should foster a deeper awareness of God's presence in the kitchen, in the family, and in the world.

"Some families set aside time on Saturday morning each week to go to the local farmers' market to pick up fresh produce. They make it a family event. They are there to shop, but they also enjoy the weather, live music, food samples, and whatever else is going on at the market that day. This is something that we do every week, and our kids love it. If, for some reason, we can't make it to the market on Saturday morning, our kids get upset. It's like they've been deprived of a treat. And everything that we do at the market is really geared toward planning our menu for the week," he explained, adding that families who cook together are better able to achieve "communion."

"Everyone's in the kitchen together. Family members are actually talking to each other. This is a great way to build community and to prepare and enjoy good food at home," he says.

PRAYER THROUGH FASTING

Catholic tradition recognizes the importance of balance, especially in spiritual life and prayer practices. So feasting at Christmas, Easter, and special holidays like St. Patrick's Day or the feast of Our Lady of Guadalupe are offset by times of fasting. There's a give-and-take in spiritual life, a recognition that life cannot and should not be a continual party. Singing must be balanced by silence, receiving must be balanced by giving, and feasting must be balanced by fasting.

Although the Church still expects believers to fast a couple times a year (on Ash Wednesday and Good Friday) and to abstain from eating meat on the Fridays of Lent, fasting has lost some of its shine in Catholic spiritual circles. For too long, it was seen as a kind of punishment, and when the Church eased restrictions on fasting and abstinence after the Second Vatican Council in the 1960s, many Catholics began to see it as something outdated and unnecessary.

Fasting is an important aspect of most of the world's great religions, including Judaism, Islam, Buddhism, and Christianity, because it's a simple physical practice that can lead to increased spiritual depth and mental clarity. We know from Scripture that Jesus went out into the desert to fast and pray, and many of the great saints over the ages incorporated this practice into their spiritual life as well. If you've ever fasted, even for a day or part of a day, you know that in addition to hearing your stomach growl, you tend to become more attuned to things around you.

In Catholic tradition, fasting can have multiple purposes. The biggest benefit is that when you create an empty space within by giving up food or some other thing that uses up your energy and attention, God often rushes in to fill the void. Fasting tends to deepen prayer experiences and open hearts and minds to the Spirit at work.

You can also use fasting as a way to align yourself with the poor and hungry. By giving up a meal or two on a regular basis, you can offer your hunger pangs in prayer for those who are hungry every day.

Walt Chura, SFO, a spiritual director and Secular Franciscan, incorporates fasting into his weekly schedule year-round. Until 5 P.M. every Friday, he eats only one slice of whole-wheat bread with peanut butter and jam for breakfast and one slice for lunch. He also continues the old-school Catholic practice of abstaining from meat every Friday of the year, and he does it all as a spiritual practice for peace. He began the practice following the suggestion of the U.S. bishops in their 1980s pastoral letter "The Challenge of Peace."

"Fasting always raises one's consciousness of the millions who go hungry every day. It makes one reflect on the geo-politics of poverty and the maldistribution of wealth, which creates enormous resentment, discontent and violent reactions among the oppressed and their allies toward the powerful of the world," Walt explains. "Fasting keeps one conscious of one's obligations toward creating a more just society and world both by personal works of mercy and promoting the common good in the social order. This is peacemaking."

He says fasting is a reminder to "go inward for the sake of compassion and to spend time with the source of compassion. This is prayer."

In his book *The Spirituality of Fasting*, Monsignor Charles Murphy explains that the Desert Fathers who lived in the Egyptian desert in the fourth and fifth centuries offered "great wisdom" through their witness to the power of fasting to enhance spiritual life and relationship with God.

"They became convinced that the condition of the body reflects the condition of the soul. An undisciplined body reveals an undisciplined soul. Body and soul have a reciprocal influence upon each other because they are dimensions of each person's identity," he writes.

Fasting, in Catholic practice, is typically linked with prayer and charity. Together they are known as the three "pillars" of Lent, the liturgical season when these aspects of spiritual life get the most attention, although they're meant to be part of Catholic life year-round.

Try moving beyond the tight parameters typically set around fasting. You don't have to fast for a whole day. You don't even necessarily have to fast from food. You can give up a main meal one day a week, known as a partial fast, or give up Facebook and Twitter one day a week or one day a month. If you want to give up one element of your diet—meat, alcohol, sugar—that's known as abstinence rather than fasting.

Find something you know gets in the way of your peace and your prayer, and see what happens when you eliminate it for a set period of time. If you decide you want to undertake a serious fast—a full day or more—be sure to check with your doctor first.

Practical Wisdom

If done with proper care, fasting can be a powerful practice that cleanses the body of impurities, enhances the power of the mind, sensitizes us to the needs of the spirit, breaks our addictions to unhealthy eating habits, and makes a significant symbolic statement about the desire to stand against the excesses of consumer culture.

—John Michael Talbot, *The Lessons of St. Francis*

TALENT AS PRAYER TREASURE

I'm not one of those crafty people who can create visual master-pieces that make people swoon. I was one of those kids who struggled in school to make a clay pot that didn't crumple in on itself on the potter's wheel or a self-portrait that was more than a sad stick figure. Those folks who can pour out their thoughts and feelings and artistic energy through oil paint brushed across canvas, or fabric squares stitched expertly together, or cold metal pounded into soft curves leave me in awe.

I'm so intrigued by—or possibly even jealous of—artistic ability that I often switch into reporter mode when I meet someone who can do what I can't. More often than not, I learn that there's a spiritual element to these talents, which only serves to make them more awe-inspiring to me. Imagine being able to sculpt or knit or coax seeds into brilliant flowers, all while walking nearer to God.

IN THE GARDEN

Beth Dotson Brown, a writer and editor living in Lancaster, Kentucky, began gardening 20 years ago for health reasons. She didn't want to eat foods that had been treated with chemicals, so she turned to a plot of land at a community garden and raised her own.

"My faith and spirituality tell me that I must care for my body because God lives in me. Caring for my health is strongly connected to God's presence within me. I also recognized that as a writer and editor, my work is sedentary. Any habit that gets me outside and moving is good," she told me, explaining that her spiritual connection to gardening grew once she was able to have a garden in her own yard. She also became active in the nearby Franciscan Peace Center, and as she learned more about St. Francis and his connection to nature, her spiritual relationship with gardening deepened.

"I began to realize I was connecting with the very basic goodness of the earth that God created for us. He gave us these gifts of the earth to nourish and sustain us and what could be more blessed than to be a part of utilizing those gifts and nurturing all of creation, not just the people who eat the food but the very soil that the plants grow in, the life in and around the garden," she explains.

Moving Meditation

If gardening is a spiritual outlet for you, consider planting a "Mary Garden," a flower bed devoted to the Blessed Mother and filled with plants named in her honor. Some common choices include marigolds (Mary's Gold), baby's breath (Mary's Veil), bleeding heart (Mary's Heart), grape hyacinth (Church Steeples), and Lady's Mantel (Mary's Mantel). Add a Mary statue, a birdbath or fountain, and perhaps a bench or chair, and you've got the perfect outdoor sacred space.

Beth, whose dedication to gardening and healthy cooking became stronger after she was diagnosed with breast cancer at 42, told me that spirituality has always been an integral part of gardening and an integral part of the many different aspects of her life that she sees as "bundled together by the desire to live simply and focus on love."

She says gardening is a "sacred task" that allows her to give life through planting and care and at the same time provides opportunities for meditation through rhythmic movement like weeding, watering, mulching, and more.

"It's a time when I remember those in prayer who are in need. I usually begin with an Our Father for one person, a Hail Mary for someone else. Then it becomes more of a conversation with God that meanders to wherever the Holy Spirit is leading me that day," she said. "I typically feel refreshed afterward, almost like I feel after a good confession."

You don't need a plot of land or even a green thumb to get some spiritual benefits from gardening. I haven't been able to produce a single zucchini or string bean in my many failed attempts at vegetable gardening, yet I often seek out the peaceful, meditative opportunities that await me in my suburban backyard in all but the harshest winter months.

I've been known to disappear into flower beds and patches of perennials for hours at a time, lost in the rhythm—and satisfaction—of pulling out hungry weeds by their tangled roots and creating space for plants and flowers to grow. With dirt under my nails and sweat streaming down my neck, I feel closer to God and settle into a silent place of expectant waiting.

Notes from the Journey

I always have three big pots of basil and parsley growing outside my back door during the summer months. There's definitely a sacred element to this small brush with growing my own food. As I pinch the leaves and swish them around in the salad spinner, I breathe deep of the strong basil scent that lingers on my hands and fills my kitchen. It's like a culinary version of incense, rising toward heaven and lifting my heart and spirit.

I chop the basil and mix it with garlic, cheese, pine nuts, and olive oil until it becomes the pesto sauce my children love so much. They've actually been known to cheer when they walk into the kitchen and get a powerful whiff of the mixture sitting beside a pot of boiling water, just waiting to be poured out over some penne. We even freeze at least a dozen containers at the end of summer to see us through the long basil-less winter.

Taking something from planter to plate feeds my desire to go farther with my gardening, to learn more, and to become God's co-creator in bringing nourishing goodness into the world. It's like my own little slice of Eden.

KNIT ONE, PRAY TOO

If the great outdoors isn't your thing, plenty of indoor opportunities exist for prayerful artistic expression. In fact, prayer shawl ministries are growing in popularity among Catholic parishes, giving members the opportunity to combine their talents and their faith in a communal experience that fosters friendship, service, and mutual support.

Marilyn Schwasta first got involved in a knitting ministry through a difficult personal experience. Her father had numerous cardiac issues and was always cold, so Marilyn found a pattern in a book called *The Prayer Shawl Ministry* and began work on a gift for him. One month later, her father was admitted to the hospital with a dire prognosis.

"I was knitting like a fiend to finish the shawl and praying constantly as I was knitting. Unfortunately twelve days later and home on hospice, he passed away. My mom and sister and I were very grateful to God that he didn't suffer long so really, our prayers were answered," Marilyn told me. "I, however, somehow felt that I could 'save Dad' if I had finished the shawl. So it was three-quarters completed and I put it aside; I couldn't even look at it for a while."

Eventually, Marilyn read more about prayer shawl ministry and decided that her sister, Karen, would love the shawl she'd started for their father. She gave it to her with the following note:

> Dear Karen,
>
> I think Dad would want you to have the enclosed. When you put it on, think of him wrapping his arms around you and saying, "I love you." He must have been very proud of his nurse daughter that last week. You protected his dignity, kept him comfortable, and let him stand by his decision to go home. Your love set him free. No father could be prouder.
>
> Love always,
> Marilyn

When Marilyn saw the comfort and peace the shawl brought to her sister, she decided to start a ministry to do the same for others. In 2010, she began with a goal of making shawls and lap blankets for those on the parish's prayer list and for spouses or parents who had suffered a loss. The ministry has grown to include baptismal shawls, prayer cloths for confirmation candidates, scarves for youth group graduates going off to college, blankets to celebrate special occasions such as milestone birthdays or anniversaries, and baby blankets for "Life Choice," a group that assists young mothers who have made the decision to keep their babies.

"We have ten active members, meeting once a month. We sometimes meet in the parish center and will also meet in our homes," Marilyn says, explaining that members take turns leading prayers at the beginning and end of each gathering. "Our knitting time is somewhat informal, as we have less experienced members who need help with their project. However, we do have periods of quiet time, which just seem to happen, where you just hear the clicking of needles, and that is when we pray individually. Before the final prayer we have special intentions."

Marilyn admitted that when first learning to knit, it can be tough to concentrate on anything but the pattern and stitches, but with time, it gets easier and the rhythm lends itself to prayer. Similar prayer opportunities exist for those who crochet or quilt or embroider. In the steady and deliberate movement of needle and thread or wool, prayers can be woven into the silence and even in the cloth itself.

I met Marilyn after a talk I gave at a women's retreat. She came over to me and gave me a small knitted prayer cloth to place in my sacred space at home. I was so touched by her kindness. But more than that, I was awed by the movement of the Spirit. Marilyn walked into my life the day before I was about to begin this section of this chapter, reminding me that when I open myself to God and others through prayer, I often get exactly what I need, usually when I don't even know what it is I need.

ARTISTIC EXPRESSION

Obviously cooking, gardening, and knitting are just a few of the many creative pursuits that can include prayer. I know some artists who pray as they paint. I once interviewed an artist who would put on spiritual or classical music and allow the movement of the music to guide her brush and her prayers. The results were these beautiful visual expressions of what was happening through song and spirit.

I know a blacksmith who can usually be found pounding away at glowing hot metal outside our parish's craft fair each November. Sitting in my sacred space is a cross he brandished and set into a piece of marble that was once part of my local church's altar rail. The proceeds for the crosses went to our parish school, bringing his hobby and his spiritual life together in an act of charity.

Whatever your interest or skill or talent, begin to look at it from a new angle. Is there a way to weave prayer into the movement? Is there an opportunity to use your talent not only as a creative and spiritual outlet but as a service to others as well?

TAKING GOD TO WORK

Most people spend the better part of every day at work and getting to and from work. If work and prayer life are kept completely separate, you could very well lose out on prime prayer time. That doesn't mean you're going to start saying the Rosary out loud in your office or on the subway. Bringing spirituality into the workplace is focused on more subtle displays of faith.

ON THE COMMUTE

First let's look at how you get to work. Do you drive your car? Ride a bus or train? Walk? Whatever your answer, you can find easy ways to add prayer to the mix.

Driving lends itself to so many options. You can play a CD of spiritual music or even a CD of the Rosary being prayed aloud and sing or pray along. In your car, with no one else to listen in, you can even pray out loud. Any other drivers who notice will probably just think you're talking to someone on your Bluetooth.

Obviously, if you're behind the wheel, you can't do anything that requires you to read or close your eyes, so praying on the drive to and from work requires a prayer you know by heart or something that needs no words at all.

When I returned from my first silent retreat several years ago, I realized that my automatic response upon getting into the car was to turn up the radio. *Loud.* I wasn't listening to anything spiritual, mostly the classic rock channel on my satellite radio. The experience of silence on retreat prompted me to give it a try while driving. Instead of singing all the way to and from my daughter's preschool, I turned off the radio and allowed myself to sink into the quiet of my little makeshift chapel on wheels. Suddenly, the 15 minutes spent driving became refreshing rather than depleting. I'd return home to my basement office feeling as though I'd already had my prayer time. Even now, when life feels beyond crazy, a quiet car is the perfect place to listen to what I might be missing when I'm surrounded by noise and other people.

If you take public transportation, praying during the commute becomes even easier. You can use your smartphone to pray with one of the many apps designed for on-the-go prayer, you can bring along a prayer book or spiritual reading, or you can close your eyes and slip away into a much more peaceful place. Just hold onto your purse if you're closing your eyes on a subway.

During Lunch Hour

Before I became a home-based writer, I spent many years behind a desk, sometimes in a little cubicle, in various newspaper offices. And more often than not, I ate my lunch in front of my computer so I could continue working on a story while mindlessly munching something unhealthy.

Every once in a while, however, on a beautiful day, I'd step outside and walk to a park or people-watch from an outdoor bench or visit a nearby church. What a difference that short respite made in the rest of my workday.

If you work at a desk or in a workplace that requires you to be stationary for hours at a time, try to find at least a few minutes to get up and get away, not only for your prayer life but for your health, too. Sitting in one place for too many hours isn't good for your heart or your soul.

Maybe you're lucky enough to work close to a neighborhood church. If so, check the schedule to see if you can get to Mass during lunch hour or even before work. Many "commuter parish" priests are adept at completing a daily Mass in 25 minutes, leaving you plenty of time to grab a quick bite afterward.

If that's not an option, simply stop in and light a candle for someone you love or sit before the Blessed Sacrament for 5 minutes before heading to the local food vendor cart to pick up your favorite sandwich.

Chances are good your workplace isn't near a church. In that case, you'll have to get a little more creative. Find a nice park, a museum, or even an empty conference room or other unused corner of your office building where you can get some uninterrupted silence and solitude. If you absolutely can't leave your desk, try to block out the noise around you and pray silently for just a few minutes. You can even visit an online prayer space (check Appendix C for links) and get the spiritual inspiration you need right where you are.

If possible, bring a few items that give your workspace a sacred aura. It doesn't have to be a cross or statue of a saint, if that's something that would cause problems for you at work. It can be a photograph of a place that makes you think of God's goodness, a quote or poem hung near your computer, or a religious item kept in your desk drawer where you can see it when you need it. (I talk a lot more about creating sacred spaces in the next chapter.)

Moving Meditation

Back in the "old days," Catholics typically prayed the Angelus at 6 A.M., noon, and 6 P.M. To this day, you may still hear church bells ringing out the prayer time despite the fact that this practice is unfamiliar to many post–Vatican II Catholics. It's a simple prayer, however, and one that can easily fit into your lunch hour prayer routine. Stop what you're doing at noon, maybe even set your phone or watch to chime at that hour, and say this Scripture-based Marian prayer. (I explain it in depth in Appendix A.)

In an Endless Meeting

So much of your workday is probably spent tied up in meetings, running to appointments, beating deadlines, and facing other stress-inducing responsibilities. What's so prayerful about that? Well, nothing, really, but you can bring your own brand of on-the-go spirituality to even the most difficult work moments.

While sitting in a meeting that drones on and on, watching the clock tick minute by minute, silently whisper short "aspirations" like the Jesus Prayer—Lord Jesus Christ, Son of God, have mercy on me, a sinner—as you struggle to stay awake … or stay out of the latest office argument.

When you're confronted with a difficult co-worker, boss, client, student, or customer, turn the tables. Instead of cursing under your breath, pray for the person who is making your work life miserable. Ask God to bless him or her and to bring peace to your dealings, to give you the willingness to recognize the child of God beneath the difficult exterior.

As you complete a deadline task, take a 2-minute break before starting something else to thank God for your ability to do your job. Also ask for the grace to carry on with whatever is coming next. Again, if you can, get up and walk around, even if it's just around the floor of your building. You'd be surprised at how it can help your physical, mental, and spiritual health.

If you do more physically taxing labor all day—standing at a cash register, working a jackhammer, waiting on tables, running after preschoolers—reverse the plan and use your short breaks to sit, unmoving, in silence. Keeping up a frantic physical pace can burn you out emotionally and spiritually, so you need to be sure to recharge throughout the workday, even if it's just to say your favorite prayer and surrender all your tensions into God's hands.

Practical Wisdom

Why would we want to look for God in our work? The simplest answer is that most of us spend so much of our time working that it would be a shame if we couldn't find God there. A more complex reason is that there is a creative energy in work that is somehow tied to God's creative energy.

—Gregory F. Pierce, *Spirituality of Work*

USING TECHNOLOGY TO PRAY

The high-tech gadgets and systems that have made our lives easier—smartphones, email, texting, and more—can come at a price, not just in dollars and cents but in silence and sanity. People are connected 24/7, making every waking moment an opportunity for constant communication. Even during the night and on vacation, emails and texts pile up.

From a spirituality standpoint, it would seem that technology has no place in a life of prayer. But as with most things in this life, the key is balance. To be sure, you need to turn off all the bells and whistles, dings and vibrations now and then and simply break the high-tech connection. It's the only way to experience true, deep silence and contemplation.

On the flip side, however, is a world of prayer potential at your fingertips—literally. Through social networking, blogs, tweets, and more, you can access all sorts of prayer guides and inspirational words, music, and images to boost your spiritual experience. Even outlets like Facebook can provide opportunities for meeting other spiritual seekers who will pray with you and for you from across the ether of the internet. Seek and you will find. That's certainly the case when it comes to online prayer possibilities.

I use several digital prayer prompts. Every morning, when I open my inbox, I find an email from the Word of God Everyday, a free online subscription that provides me with a daily email that includes a short Scripture quote, a one-line related reflection by a saint or other holy person, and a stunning photograph. Even when my email inbox is overflowing, I look forward to what's coming in this daily spiritual jolt and usually save it for last so I can savor whatever message appears.

I have also made many spiritual friends—those friends who connect with me on a soul level—through social networking, where we trade spiritual blog links, quotes, and prayerful support throughout the day. It's not unusual for me to have multiple friends in need of prayers on any given day. There, in the seemingly faceless world of Facebook, I have made new spiritual connections, a few of which have gone on to become real-life soul friends as well.

Start to use technology to your spiritual advantage. Find a few blogs that speak to your soul. Use email and social networking to reach out to friends who share your hunger for a deeper connection with God. Text or email an uplifting message to someone who is ill or going through a tough time. Begin to build a virtual spiritual community that feeds your real-life journey.

Just be sure you don't get too wrapped up in your virtual life, spiritual and otherwise. It's easy to replace face-to-face friendships and in-depth prayer with virtual versions, but you need both. Always remember balance. Step away from the screen on a regular basis to keep your center. Fast from technology now and then to break bad habits and give yourself a chance to experience life without the distractions.

GOING FORWARD ...

† Infuse your meals with a sense of the sacred by bringing prayer into your cooking, kitchen environment, and mealtime rituals.

† Any hobby or talent is fertile ground for everyday prayer when you approach it from a place of mindfulness and begin to recognize God in the details.

† Bringing an element of spirituality into your workday can transform the daily grind into an opportunity for love, forgiveness, compassion, and joy.

† You can use technology to your benefit by creating a balance of virtual and real prayer experiences through social networking, email, and other high-tech options.

6

SOUNDS AND SIGNS OF THE SPIRIT

Certain things are likely to put you in a spiritual frame of mind without any effort on your part—a piece of classical music perfectly performed, a grand cathedral with spires reaching heavenward, a brilliant sunset that catches you by surprise as you drive home from work, a delicate orchid hanging just so from a long and graceful branch. Suddenly it's as though you're standing toe-to-toe with God.

Those inspiring moments are probably few and far between. Much more likely is the uneventful drive past ordinary looking churches amid dandelion-spotted lawns. Although God is no less present there, it isn't as easy to feel him in such ordinary surroundings. Hence the need or desire for sacred spaces, those beautiful places or spiritual touchstones that help us mere humans make that enormous leap toward the divine.

SACRED SPACES AND SACRAMENTALS

People seek out churches and monasteries for prayer and worship because the physical surroundings help turn their thoughts toward heaven. It's hard to ignore the Spirit when you're kneeling in an old church with sun streaming through stained-glass windows and candles flickering in dark corners. Even if you're distracted, the

Spirit will keep poking you (figuratively, of course) in an effort to draw you away from all your earthly concerns and help you set your sights on God.

You don't have to hunt down an historic church to get a little of that old-time religion, however. You can bring elements of the sacred— known as "sacramentals"—into your "normal" life to create prayerful environments in less-than-prayerful places.

INCENSE AND CANDLES

There's nothing like the sight of candles and the smell of incense to get those spiritual juices flowing. For Catholics, especially, those items go hand-in-hand with the church experience.

Candles are used because they symbolize Jesus Christ, who is the "light of the world" (John 8:12), and they're meant to remind us that God is still present in the world today. When you kneel down beside the red vigil candles and light one for a friend, it's as though you're leaving behind a visible reminder of your prayer offered up to God.

Outside of Mass on particular Sundays or special liturgical celebrations, incense is more typically associated with yoga studios or New Age spirituality, but this prayer aid plays a role in Catholic spirituality as well. There's a reason incense crosses faith traditions. It not only infuses a space with a scent of the sacred, but its perfumed smoke rising to heaven is meant to symbolize prayers rising up to God.

Bringing these two elements into your everyday prayer life can help set a sacred tone in otherwise ordinary or hectic surroundings. Candles are an obvious choice, especially because they're already part of home prayer practices through the Advent wreath. Consider adding a candle to your dinner table, your nightstand, or some other place where you spend time in prayer. Opt for a battery-powered candle if you're concerned about fire. I've got several, and they're remarkably lifelike, with a faint vanilla scent and a subtle flicker.

I also burn incense at home, so much so that my husband bought it in bulk for me last Christmas. (I think it will take me at least a decade to work my way through all of it!) Sometimes I light incense even when I'm not sitting down to prayer. The air tinged with its soft scent creates a peaceful aura in my space, putting me in a more centered frame of mind, whether I'm settling down for meditation or writing on a tight deadline.

Practical Wisdom

Let my prayer be like incense before you;
my uplifted hands an evening sacrifice.

—Psalm 141:2

STATUES, ICONS, AND MORE

A few years ago, I had my heart set on a statue of Our Lady of Guadalupe for my backyard, but everything I found online was too expensive or just not my taste. Then one afternoon, when I needed to pick up some craft supplies for my kids at our local Walmart, I wheeled my cart around the end of the aisle and came face-to-face with a brightly colored version of the Patroness of the Americas, a.k.a., the Blessed Mother.

I pulled her down from her perch and loaded her into my cart. You should have seen the confused looks I got from the rest of the Walmart shoppers as I continued throwing groceries and other sundries into my cart with Mary peering down at everyone.

She now resides in a flower bed set among some mighty oaks and poplars. When I sit in my sun porch or on my deck, or wash dishes at the kitchen sink under the window, I can see her in the distance. In my front yard, I've got a clay statue of St. Francis of Assisi watching peacefully over my perennials, and near our back property line, a smaller St. Francis set into a small wooden shrine marks the graves of our beloved dog and cat.

I'm not alone in my love of statues. Drive through any neighborhood with a heavy Catholic population, and you're bound to find the Blessed Mother, various angels, and favorite saints peering out from behind shrubbery and amid flowers.

Statues and stained glass, icons, and other sacramentals are often misunderstood by non-Catholics, who see them as superstitious or "idol worship," but they are nothing of the kind. These beautiful physical reminders of interior faith are designed to lead you closer to Christ.

When you see a stained-glass window of St. Clare of Assisi, for example, you can remember her life of devotion and sacrifice and be inspired to try to be more like her. When you plant a statue of the Blessed Mother in your garden, you can do so with the hope that it will serve as a constant reminder of Mary's "yes" to God and your challenge to do the same.

Icons, those ancient images that are more common in the Eastern Church today, are considered windows into heaven, pathways to prayer. They are meant to draw you into God's space, to help you make a transcendent connection. The penetrating stares and sometimes foreign-feeling images are akin to reading Scripture. An artist doesn't paint an icon but "writes" it.

Catholics have many other sacramentals at their disposal, from holy water and religious medals to prayers of blessing and relics of saints. You can pick and choose favorite items for your own sacred space.

You may want to consider hanging a holy water font next to your front door so you can bless yourself and your children as you head out to school and work each day, or you could put one at your bedroom door so you can bless yourself before bed each night. Just be warned: holy water evaporates fast. You'll need to make pretty regular trips to your parish to get holy water, which is, of course, blessed—and free. Bring an empty bottle, and ask someone at any church or shrine you visit to point you in the right direction.

Moving Meditation

If you've never prayed before an icon before, give it a try. Find one that speaks to you. I have a lovely reproduction of the famous icon by Russian iconographer Andrei Rublev known as the *Old Testament Trinity*. Another popular icon is *Christ the Pantocrater*. Put the icon in your prayer space, and sit before it. You don't pray *to* the icon but rather *in the presence* of the icon. Let your eyes soak in the icon, not for its artistic elements but for the story it tells. No words are needed here. Just sit in silence and allow the icon to become a doorway to God.

YOUR PERSONAL PRAYER SPACE

If you don't already have a specific place for prayer, it's time to create one. No matter how big or how small—even a windowsill will do—you should have a sacred space, preferably in a quiet spot, someplace where you can be alone now and then.

You might want to revamp a corner of your bedroom, especially if you pray upon getting up and just before going to sleep. Or maybe you have a room with a picture window that looks out on a peaceful scene. If all else fails, find one shelf or table you can transform.

My main sacred space is confined to two shelves of a bookcase in my basement office, sandwiched between the cat condo and video game console. It's not the most fabulous location, but it has become a peaceful oasis for me.

As its focal point, I've placed a cross made for me by my blacksmith friend mentioned earlier. Next to it is an icon of Mary and the child Jesus, a small image of St. Francis, a battery-operated candle, a seashell from a beach vacation, and a small pinecone found during a meditative walk while on retreat. The backdrop of this space is filled with my favorite spiritual books, and in front is a small incense burner.

Whenever I want to pray, I pull out a footstool that has become my "prayer bench" and sit before the cross, candle lit and incense burning. Or I sit in a chair or on my yoga mat, whatever feels best for the type of prayer I'm doing, which could be anything from the Liturgy of the Hours to silent meditation.

Look around your house for a suitable spot, and begin to make it your own. Incorporate elements that draw you to Christ, especially a cross. Have a Bible nearby as well as other spiritual books for inspiration. If you prefer to have music playing when you pray, add that. Candles, incense, holy water—whatever helps you enter into prayer is good to include, even if it's not particularly religious. My pinecone and seashells aren't sacramentals, but they remind me of places and events that have aided my spiritual journey, so they're important to my sacred space.

If you prefer to pray outdoors, set up an outside space with a bench or chair and perhaps a statue or cross as a visual focal point.

In addition to your specific sacred space, try to bring religious elements into the rest of your home, office (if appropriate), car, or yard. When you're bringing prayer into everyday activities, it helps if you have those constant reminders to pull you back to your spiritual center when you start to slip. It could be a simple cross hanging in your kitchen, or a sign that says "Peace" hanging over your desk, or a Scripture verse printed off your computer and taped to a bathroom mirror. It doesn't have to be elaborate; it just has to speak to you.

Notes from the Journey

If you took one look at the small extra bag I'm bringing with me on vacation, you would swear I'm going on retreat and not to the New Jersey Shore with its miles of sandy beaches, boardwalk rides, and fried Oreos.

Here's what I've got in my bag: a Bible; the latest issue of *Magnificat*; *Praying the Psalms* by Thomas Merton; *Introduction to the Devout Life* by St. Francis de Sales; a blank journal; *Come to the Quiet: The Principles of Christian Meditation* by John Michael Talbot; *A Retreat with Brother Lawrence and the Russian Pilgrim* by Kerry Walters; *No Moment too Small: Rhythms of Silence, Prayer and Holy Reading* by Norvene Vest; and *Food Matters: A Guide to Conscious Eating* by Mark Bittman, lest you think I'm taking only spiritual reading.

In addition, I'm packing my trusty battery-powered candle, an icon, and a small cross. I have to skip the incense, unless I want to get myself voted off the island.

I will most likely never get to most of this. Some of it won't even make it out of my bag. Other things will get a cursory glance. But there is a chance—and a good chance—that at least one thing will strike a chord and give me some much-needed spiritual food for thought.

A portable sacred space is always part of my packing equation, whether I'm going to a monastery or Disney World.

Finding God in Nature

Blessed Pope John Paul II was known for his love of nature and the great outdoors. During the years of his papacy, before his illness limited his mobility, the world was often treated to photos of him hiking in the mountains or walking along the shores of a peaceful lake. He was even known to sneak off *incognito* to ski in the mountains of Italy, unnoticed by the Swiss Guard and unrecognized by the locals.

In his general audience on January 26, 2000, Pope John Paul II specifically addressed the significance of nature and all of God's creation in a spiritual life:

> Nature thus becomes a gospel which speaks to us of God: "from the greatness and beauty of created things comes a corresponding perception of their Creator" (*Wis* 13:5). Paul teaches us that "ever since the creation of the world [God's] invisible nature, namely, his eternal power and deity, has been clearly perceived in the things that have been made" (*Rom* 1:20). But this capacity for contemplation and knowledge, this discovery of a transcendent presence in created things must lead us also to rediscover our kinship with the earth, to which we have been linked since our own creation (cf. *Gn* 2:7). This is precisely the

goal which the Old Testament wished for the Hebrew Jubilee, when the land was at rest and man
ate what the fields spontaneously gave him (cf. *Lv*
25:11–12). If nature is not violated and degraded,
it once again becomes man's sister.

In other words, Catholics are not only called to appreciate nature
and stand in awe of God's creation; Catholics are called to care for
that creation and live in solidarity with it. Your prayer life, then, can
become the pathway to a deeper understanding of and appreciation
for the wonder of the world around you.

Practical Wisdom

Do not mock anything God has created. All creation is simple, plain
and good. And God is present throughout his creation. Why do you ever
consider things beneath your notice? God's justice is to be found in every
detail of what he has made. The human race alone is capable of injustice.
Human beings alone are capable of disobeying God's laws, because they
try to be wiser than God.

—Hildegarde von Bingen, twelfth-century mystic

APPRECIATING THE LANDSCAPE

When I'm sitting on the beach, staring out at the Atlantic Ocean, I
can't help but hear prayers of praise echoing in my head along with
the crashing waves. The power of the ocean is unsettling and comforting all at once, and for me, there's something deeply spiritual
about that.

The endless beauty, stretching out to the horizon line, is a glimmer
of eternity. The soft sand wiped clean of our footprints as the water
rushes back to the sea is a reminder of just how fleeting life on this
earth really is. The joy on my children's faces as they ride the waves
or collect shells in a bucket or follow a seagull along the water's
edge is like prayer in motion as I watch them revel in what God has
made.

And every time I sit with my toes in the sand and recognize the
stunning power of what's right in front of me, I hear the words of
Daniel 3:57–82:

> Bless the Lord, all you works of the Lord,
> praise and exalt him above all forever ...

> Angels of the Lord, bless the Lord.
> You heavens, bless the Lord.
> All you waters above the heavens, bless the Lord.
> All you hosts of the Lord, bless the Lord.
> Sun and moon, bless the Lord.
> Stars of heaven, bless the Lord.
> Shower and dew, bless the Lord.
> All you winds, bless the Lord.
> Fire and heat, bless the Lord.
> Cold and chill, bless the Lord.
> Dew and rain, bless the Lord.
> Frost and chill, bless the Lord.
> Ice and snow, bless the Lord.
> Nights and days, bless the Lord.
> Light and darkness, bless the Lord.
> Lightnings and clouds, bless the Lord.
> Let the earth bless the Lord,
> praise and exalt him above all forever.

> Mountains and hills, bless the Lord.
> Everything growing on earth, bless the Lord.
> You springs, bless the Lord.
> Seas and rivers, bless the Lord.
> You dolphins and all water creatures, bless the
> Lord.
> All you birds of the air, bless the Lord.
> All you beasts, wild and tame, bless the Lord.

> You sons of men, bless the Lord ...
> praise and exalt him above all forever.

You'll find that same sentiment echoed in the words of St. Francis of Assisi, who wrote *The Canticle of Brother Sun*, a spiritual ode to everything God created, from the sun and wind to fire and death. St. Francis is a favorite of animal lovers, environmentalists, ecologists, and gardeners because he was so thoroughly connected to the innate beauty and goodness of all God's creation.

Keep in mind that Daniel and Francis aren't just talking about those majestic views of oceans and mountaintops, sunrises and starry nights. Their love of creation was inclusive, from the galaxy above to the tiny spider underfoot. All is created by God, and, therefore, all is loved by God and bestowed with a certain goodness.

So your mission, should you decide to accept it, is to start looking at your world through rose-colored glasses. Rather than focus on the crabgrass that's ruining your lawn, marvel at the intricate beauty of the lowly dandelion. Instead of furrowing your brow in frustration when bees arrive on your picnic scene, focus on their awesome ability to gather nectar from the flowers in your yard and turn it into the golden honey that sweetens your tea.

Moving Meditation

Go outside or look out your window, and find the wonder that awaits you in nature. Reflect on the words of praise from Daniel 3:57–82 as you take time to find one thing you've never noticed before—a delicate violet growing between the cracks of a sidewalk or a glistening spider web woven between deck railings. I have an intricate mud "hut" dirt daubers built on our front porch. Although they've abandoned it, I haven't had the heart to remove it. Whenever I see it, I smile at the wonder of what God has made. See if you can find a similar treasure.

THE EYE OF THE STORM

The recent spate of unusual weather across the country and around the world—tornadoes in unlikely places, blizzards where it should be warm and heat where there should be blizzards, hail and wind and earthquakes—serves to highlight the less-beautiful and more-dangerous aspects of God's creation.

Why would God allow such violent and frightening elements into a universe he set in motion? Why not maintain a placid natural world where everything works for humanity's benefit?

The Catechism of the Catholic Church explains that God created a world that is "journeying" toward perfection, meaning it's not perfect yet. Good and evil must co-exist in this imperfect world.

"In God's plan this process of becoming involves the appearance of certain beings and the disappearance of others, the existence of the more perfect alongside the less perfect, both constructive and destructive forces of nature," the catechism states.

On a logical level, you can probably make an argument for that reasoning, but if you happen to be the person watching your home and all your belongings get washed away in a flood or torn apart in a tornado, it becomes a little more difficult. Where is God, you may wonder, when you see images of people desperate to escape a tsunami a world away or a raging wildfire in the next town?

When confronted with nature's fury, it's normal to turn to God for protection, for answers, for comfort. Special prayers have been written specifically for such occasions. When I was heading to Rome several years ago, my plane was scheduled to depart New York's JFK airport the exact time Hurricane Earl was expected to arrive there. As I headed for the airport shuttle bus in Albany, already nervous because I was going to Italy alone and hadn't been overseas in 25 years, I swore to every member of my family that if someone swooped down and offered to buy my ticket, I'd gladly bow out. I didn't want to mess with a hurricane during take-off.

But no one swooped in to take my ticket off my hands, and so I nervously arrived at my shuttle bus. Being a chatty sort, I went up to three people standing together to see if I happened to be in the right place. It turned out they, too, were going on a pilgrimage—to Lourdes, France—and they offered to watch out for me until I arrived at my Alitalia gate. But more than that, sensing my nervousness over the weather, one woman gave me her prayer book, marked to the page with "The Prayer of Blessing Against Storms."

"Christ conquers. Christ reigns. Christ orders. May Christ protect us from all storms and lightening. Christ went through their midst in peace, and the word was made flesh. Christ is with us ...," I read from the little nameless blue prayer book with the image of the *Pieta* on the cover.

As I sat on the shuttle, reading from my new prayer book and marveling at the way God intervenes in the minutia of my life, I felt a calmness descend, and I realized that my pilgrimage had already begun, right there at the shuttle bus stop. By the time we got to the airport, the skies had cleared a bit, and my flight left on time. In fact, I arrived in Rome a few minutes ahead of schedule.

God may not stop the storms, but he can see us through them.

Practical Wisdom

Earth's crammed with heaven,
And every common bush afire with God ...
—Elizabeth Barrett Browning

All Creatures, Great and Small

Sister Claire Marie Lessard, SJH, is superior of the Sisters of Jesus Our Hope in Bloomsbury, New Jersey, where Bella the dog has become part of the monastery family and routine.

About 6 years ago, the Sisters moved to their present location on a ridge in the countryside surrounded by woods, spruce trees, and a large field. Along with the beauty of God's creation came other more-frustrating parts of creation in the form of groundhogs, rabbits, deer, and mice—they caught 32 of the little critters in Have-a-Heart traps during their first year there.

"That is where Bella, our pooch, comes in. We had never had a dog, but we decided that we probably needed a little help to keep our animal friends at a distance," Sister Claire Marie told me.

A former shelter dog, Bella is a gentle 62 pounds, according to Sister Claire Marie, and friendly and quiet except when a stranger comes to the door or when any of the assorted woodland animals who share her country space dart into view.

"Our convent has a 'regularity of life' with specific times for communal and private prayer, times for communal meals, and times for recreation together. Bella is a dog that likes structure, knows our schedule, and has adapted to it quite well," says Sister Claire Marie, adding that she and the other Sisters have much to learn from their canine friend.

"She keeps her eyes on her mistress, and follows her wherever she goes. And so she reminds us of the ultimate importance of keeping our eyes on 'the Master' and following him wherever he leads us, which ultimately will be life everlasting with him in heaven," Sister Claire Marie explains. "She is also patient. She waits for someone to take her for a walk. She waits to be fed. She waits for someone to open the door to the back porch. And she waits patiently. She teaches us the value of waiting and being patient especially in this fast-track microwave society we live in."

Pets can have a special place in spiritual life. These quiet companions can sit with you while you pray in your sacred space at home or serve as protective friends who join you for a meditative walk in the evening.

Even "wild" animals can add to your spiritual life. Watching birds at the feeder in the spring or squirrels gathering acorns in the fall can give you a stronger connection to creation, to the passing of seasons, and to the circle of life of which you are a part.

Moving Meditation

Check with churches in your area to see if they host a Blessing of the Animals on or near October 4, the feast of St. Francis of Assisi. Many parishes offer blessings to household pets ranging from lizards and goldfish to ferrets and horses and everything in between. If you can't get to an official blessing, you can do one of your own. Simply sprinkle some holy water over your pet, and say a prayer. And you don't have to wait until St. Francis' feast day to use the do-it-yourself blessing. Any day is a good day to bless a beloved pet.

Praying Through Song

Most of my life has moved along as if to a soundtrack, right down to the part where people burst into song in the middle of business as usual. My mother was a singer, so our house was filled with music—Broadway show tunes, '50s music, Irish music, oldies that dated to my grandmother's youth. My mother would often bring me along on her many, many visits to various nursing homes to entertain, and inevitably I'd be up there singing "Hello, Dolly!" or some other "hit" before the evening was out.

By the time I reached junior high, I was in my parish folk group, taking singing lessons, playing guitar, and writing religious songs. I later fronted a rock 'n' roll band for quite a few years. Even now, my days are set to a changing melody, from pop or rock when I'm dancing with my girls, to instrumental or classical when I'm writing in my office, to spiritual when I'm alone in my car. The great thing about music is that there's something for every mood, every moment. When I get into my car and turn on the Christian station, even if I'm not in the most prayerful mental place, the songs remind me of God's goodness and bring me around.

Have you ever gone to Mass in a rotten mood, wondering why you're even there, thinking maybe you should have just stayed home in bed? And then you hear the choir sing a song that seems to strike at your heart, or the psalm is so perfect it brings you to tears. Music can do that like almost nothing else can. Beautiful music can rival a beautiful sunset or a perfect moon; it's a way to God.

MUSICAL BACKDROP

Jean Leonard, a cantor, parish music minister, and mom of three, has been involved in church music since she was 6 years old. Although when she first joined her parish folk group she says she saw it mainly as "fun," it didn't take long for her to realize that singing at Mass was something more.

"I do feel *strongly* that I am helping others pray. For me, prayers are enhanced—sometimes intensified, sometimes clarified, sometimes softened--when they are sung," she told me. "If I think of prayer as a connection to the whisper of the Spirit inside of all of us, which is one of the ways I think of prayer. I think sung prayer can go deeper."

Jean, who is a soprano in the choral group Albany *Pro Musica* in New York's capital city, sees her voice as a gift from God, something she's called to use in as many ways as possible, something that's as much a part of her as her hair or eye color, she says.

"It is in great part how I define myself. It is a gift. This is clear to me. It is my gift, not meant to be squandered and not meant to be hidden, and not meant to be ignored. So I sing a lot! And in many different venues, groups," Jean explains. "And what that means is that sometimes I'm singing at an Albany *Pro Musica* rehearsal and the 'prayer' of the piece moves me so much that I am praying right then and there, in the midst of a secular choir rehearsal."

I've had the privilege of hearing Jean sing at church many times, and every time, I feel as though she's singing right to me. In fact, the first time I heard her sing, I told my husband, "If I die, I want Jean to sing at my funeral." I can't think of a better way to leave this world than to be sung out by Jean, who was hesitant to offer any "spiritual advice" when I asked her, but gave the following suggestions for weaving music into prayer:

"Music moves me. It gets inside of me and changes something in there. And I know that happens for people who aren't 'musical,' but are music lovers. I guess I would say listen. Really listen. If praying in silence is difficult—for me it is virtually impossible—add music. Add an orchestral piece that you love, or add some acoustic guitar that keeps you calm, or add George Winston playing his piano. It doesn't matter what the music is," she says. "It matters that the music moves you. God is in that. There's not a lot I'm sure of, but I'm sure of that."

Practical Wisdom

He who sings prays twice.
—St. Augustine

Move to Your Own Beat

You don't have to sing church hymns or even listen to classical music to get a spiritual lift from a song. Many secular songs probably move you in interior ways. Whatever music inspires you to reflect or go inward, use it to deepen your prayer life.

If you're going on a long car ride, make a mix of music that speaks to your soul, and use it as the soundtrack for your drive. If you know you're going to be stuck at the airport for a long layover, put some soul-soothing music on your MP3 player and disappear into your own world as everyone else watches the clock and impatiently taps their feet. Use music to bring prayer into unlikely places.

I'm sometimes stunned by the power of music to move me, even when I feel closed down or spiritually empty. And it doesn't have to be a brilliant classical piece. Sometimes the most stripped-down chant, sung *a cappella*, is all I need. I remember one such moment when I was on retreat at the Abbey of the Genesee near Rochester,

New York. It was my first time attending Night Prayer with the monks, and as they ended their prayers in the darkened stone chapel, they all turned to face an icon of the Blessed Mother with the child Jesus. With the lights out and only a few candles burning under the icon, the church took on a haunting but soothing glow. The monks then chanted the *Salve Regina* (Hail Holy Queen) in Latin.

Although I'd been at the retreat house since earlier that afternoon and had even prayed Evening Prayer with the monks, I felt as though my retreat began with that praying of the *Salve Regina*. It was so powerful, it shook me to my core. Suddenly, all the worries I'd carried along with me on the 4-hour drive melted away, and I entered into the moment.

Moving Meditation

Step outside your musical comfort zone. Find a piece or style of music that's new to you—an instrumental piece, an old sacred song, opera, jazz, a concerto, or maybe a rock song with inspiring lyrics. Play the song once through to see how it feels. Now settle into a comfortable position, close your eyes, and listen again. Does it feel different? Do you hear things you didn't hear before? Begin to note the songs that move you spiritually, and add them to your home collection little by little. Before you know it, you'll have a spiritual soundtrack for those times when silent prayer just won't do.

OUTWARD SIGNS OF INWARD MOVEMENT

When you immerse yourself in a life of everyday prayer, you're likely to find that your desire to serve others begins to increase. Prayer tends to do that; it opens you up, first to God, then to yourself, then to others.

Service, or charity, is an integral part of a Catholic prayer life. Faith must move out into the world so it becomes more than just reverent words and gestures. Prayer must become compassionate actions lived daily, as Jesus himself taught:

> For I was hungry and you gave me food, I was thirsty and you gave me drink, a stranger and you welcomed me ... Amen, I say to you, whatever you did for one of these least brothers of mine, you did for me. (Matthew 25:35–40)

SERVICE AS PRAYER

In her book *A Willing Heart: How to Serve When You Think You Can't*, author Marci Alborghetti talks about the struggles Christians sometimes face as they attempt to bring the words of their faith alive through the details of their daily actions.

"Often it can seem impossible to overcome our human nature and act according to the spark of divine nature God placed within us. The odds are against it. That is, if we act alone," she writes. "Fortunately, we don't have to. Grace is our bit of divine nature, our little bit—as it were—of heaven. Grace is God's way of making it possible to accept his invitation to serve, and grace is what gives us the knowledge that God will protect us and guide us as we serve."

I know people for whom service is such a natural outgrowth of their spiritual lives they exude a kind of peacefulness at all times. They live in a simple and stripped-down house, they protest wars, and they visit third-world countries during their vacations.

Truly living out the Gospel is a radical spirituality. You may find contemporary Catholics who witness to it, and you may find favorite saints whose lives were defined by it—Francis of Assisi or Blessed Mother Teresa of Calcutta, for example. But this kind of living is not for the faint of heart. Then again, Jesus never said it would be easy.

Practical Wisdom

The whole idea of compassion is based on a keen awareness of the interdependence of all these living beings, which are all part of one another, and all involved with one another.

—Thomas Merton

When the rich official asked Jesus what he must do to have eternal life, Jesus told him to keep the commandments. When the man said he had kept the commandments since his youth, Jesus responded with the line that probably makes most Christians shudder:

> There is still one thing left for you: sell all that
> you have and distribute it to the poor, and you
> will have a treasure in heaven. Then come, follow
> me. (Luke 18:22)

Wow. If *that's* what we have to do to gain eternal life, what chance do most of us have? Although some are called to give up everything they own and serve the poor, most people are providing for themselves and their families, just trying to get by one day at a time. What are they supposed to do?

When you look at this passage in relation to your spiritual life, you have to put it all in perspective. You probably can't give away everything, but chances are good you can give up some things. And perhaps more importantly, you can give up your *attachment* to the things that distract you from Gospel living, whether it's the extra high-tech gadgets, the daily frappucinos, or the obsession with working out.

I talk a lot more about simplicity and detachment in Chapter 7, but those topics come into play here as well. It's easy to throw money at a problem, tossing $20 into the collection basket or sending a check to an organization that cares for poor children in another country. Much harder is changing your life in ways that plant the seeds of service before you ever set foot in a soup kitchen or sign up to help with a Habitat for Humanity project. And those seeds grow out of prayer. Without prayer, service is simply philanthropy. With prayer, service is charity. And charity is the Gospel come to life.

John Michael Talbot is a musician, author, and founder of the Brothers and Sisters of Charity, a Franciscan-based religious community of celibate members, families, and single lay Catholics. In his book, *The Lessons of St. Francis: How to Bring Simplicity and Spirituality into Your Daily Life*, he reminds readers that although Francis devoted hours each day to prayer, his faith was not confined to a chapel.

"Most Christians celebrate the Incarnation of Christ as man around Christmastime and ignore it for the rest of the year. But for Francis, the Incarnation served as a minute-by-minute reminder to be deeply involved in the world, loving people at close range instead of from inside the strong, stony walls of a monastery," he writes, explaining that spirituality that focuses only on self is missing the bigger part.

"Spiritual growth leads directly to service. Spirituality that doesn't is stunted and incomplete," he writes.

Begin to see prayer as a pathway to service. Pray that God will open your eyes and your heart to people and organizations in need of your help. It doesn't have to be something monumental, like traveling to another state or country to work with the poor on a long-term basis. It can be something as simple as helping with food pantry collections at your parish, knitting shawls for nursing home residents, or making a meal for a family who has just welcomed home a newborn and may be under more stress than usual.

Notes from the Journey

Sometimes, when I'm yelling at my children for yelling at each other, I realize how ridiculous I must sound. Surely even my 6-year-old must be wondering why it's okay for Mommy to yell, but it's not okay for her to yell.

When I take the time to reflect on what I try to teach my children about the way they should talk, the way they should act, and the way they should strive to live, I have to admit I may be doing a whole lot of preaching. But practicing? Not so much. Which is too bad because, as they say, actions speak louder than words.

It would be easy to look at the big picture and pat myself on the back for my general behavior out in the world each day, but can I say the same thing about my behavior among my family each day? Sometimes it's easier to love and "serve" a stranger in a far-off land than it is to love and serve the people living alongside us. The stranger doesn't talk back or mess up the house. The stranger can be kept at arm's length.

Jesus doesn't invite us to love at a distance. He invites us to love as we want to be loved. Easy to preach, pretty to quote, but difficult to live.

Mother Teresa once said, "What can you do to promote world peace? Go home and love your family." So begin there, right where you are today. Service starts in your home and expands outward to your parish, your community, and eventually the world at large.

Don't be overwhelmed by the idea of service. It doesn't have to be scary or all-encompassing. Just pray for grace and guidance, and you'll be led to those who need your help, even if they happen to be just in the next room.

PRAYING WITH OTHERS

Every prayer life benefits from communal prayer, whether it's said around the family dinner table, at Mass on Sunday, on retreat, or spontaneously among friends. When we join our hearts and minds in prayer, that prayer seems to resonate a little deeper, rippling outward to touch others.

Once when I was on retreat, we went around the room and prayed out loud for someone in need or for ourselves. It was so powerful as we listened to each other's special intentions and then quietly prayed together. The experience was intense, almost palpable, as if the prayers had physical vibrations that could be felt moving around the room.

Not every communal prayer experience is going to be so extreme, but joining with others in prayer opens doors you might not have noticed before. Prayer is an intimate sharing, and it can bring people together in unexpected ways for the good of others. Although prayer itself doesn't seem like "service," it most definitely is when we use it to pray for those in need, or for world peace, or for any number of needs larger than our own.

My 11-year-old daughter and I recently had an opportunity to visit a Carmelite cloister where the nuns leave only to go to doctor appointments. Their entire lives are spent praying for others. It can be a difficult life choice to understand. Why not go out and serve the poor or teach school or care for the sick? But theirs is a singular focus: prayer. Everything they do, from their chores to their work, to their actual prayer time is offered up for others.

Praying with others takes prayer to a whole new dimension, which can, in turn, positively affect your private prayer life.

Spiritual Companions

When you open your spiritual life beyond your own world, chances are good you'll meet people who connect with you in a deep way. These are spiritual friends—soul mates of sorts—and they'll be important companions on your journey.

You may already have one or two people in your life who rise to this level, people who may share your interests or sense of humor but even more than that, share your hunger for God. You may find the most likely spiritual friends right within your own family: your spouse, a parent, a child, or a sibling. But you can also find and nurture spiritual friendships among those you meet in your parish or at the office or at the health club.

When writing my book, *Walking Together: Discovering the Catholic Tradition of Spiritual Friendship*, I had the good fortune of talking to many people who have benefited and grown from these kinds of friendships. I've been blessed with quite a few in my own life. My faith life has been shaped and strengthened by those spiritual friends who have shared their own stories and struggles, who come to my aid with prayers and spiritual encouragement, who pray with me and for me even when we're separated by hundreds of miles.

Begin to look at some of the close friendships in your life. Do you have any friends who share your love of God and want to pursue a life of deeper prayer? Think about how you can encourage this friendship. There are any number of ways to get started: go for a walking Rosary meditation together, read the same spiritual book and then get together to discuss it, visit a sacred site together, attend Mass together on certain days, or maybe even go on retreat together. Any one of these or countless other possibilities will strengthen your friendship and your faith and help both of you move forward on your spiritual paths.

Moving Meditation

Think of one person who has had an impact on your spiritual life. Get out some paper or a nice card, and write a letter to this friend. Don't just cover the normal niceties —How are you? How's the family? How's the weather? This letter needs to go deeper. Let your friend know how much you value what he or she has done to help you grow closer to God. Letter-writing is a lost art in our modern world, but a personal letter is sure to bring a smile to your friend's face. Make an effort to write one personal letter each month to a friend with whom you have a spiritual connection.

GOING FORWARD ...

† Create a sacred space in your home, a place where you can retreat in silence and solitude for regular prayer.

† Nature can be a perfect conduit for spiritual experiences. Look for God's presence in the beauty of the world around you.

† Use music—sacred or secular—to inspire your prayer, especially during those times when you can't pray silently.

† Spiritual growth is meant to move outward. Through regular everyday prayer, you are likely to experience an increased desire to serve others.

7

SILENCE, SIMPLICITY, AND SOLITUDE

St. Benedict of Nursia, the father of Western monasticism, began the prologue of his "Rule"—the same Rule that continues to guide the majority of monastics today— with the following challenge:

> Listen with the ear of your heart.

You may look at your life right now and imagine it's so much crazier than a life of prayer lived centuries ago, but St. Benedict's 1,500-year-old Rule reminds us that when it comes to human weakness and human struggles, the core issues remain the same, no matter how the world changes.

Life can get the best of you. Life can leave you gasping for breath and racing through your days without really listening. Life needs a pause button.

SETTING LIFE TO A SACRED RHYTHM

The Rule of St. Benedict remains relevant all these centuries later because it hit on something central to spiritual life. Without God as its focus, life quickly unravels—and with it all your hopes for serenity.

With a few minor adjustments, however, you can bring a spiritual movement to your own life, even without the benefit of a quiet monastery. You can nurture a peaceful presence in your own home, your own schedule, your own skin by marking certain moments, hours, days, and events with a moveable feast of prayer.

LESSONS FROM THE MONASTICS

The Benedictine maxim *ora et labora*, "pray and work," serves as a template for monastics everywhere, reminding monks and nuns that life must be lived with balance. This just as easily can be applied to the lives of people out in the world—people like you. Your life should not be all work or all prayer or all play or *all* anything. Too much of anything, even a good thing, isn't necessarily healthy. The Benedictine model of spirituality is one of moderation.

For the monastic, life moves to the same rhythm day after day: prayer, work, prayer, meals, prayer, sacred reading, prayer, recreation, prayer, sleep. Prayer is like a beautiful refrain that sets the tone for the day. When prayer becomes so regular, so pervasive, it begins to change the way you encounter the nonprayer aspects of your day. Prayer makes you more open to life's many demands by infusing them with purpose, love, and service.

"Prayer welcomes work," says Sister Elizabeth Matz, a Benedictine Sister of Pittsburgh. "If we are receptive and willing, work creates the attitude of hospitality. This hospitality underlies Benedict's design of the rhythm of prayer and work. This rhythm becomes a support for reflective prayer and contemplation, which relieves stress and anxiety."

It's all well and good to say you can live like a Benedictine at home or in the grocery store or at work. But you and I both know that without the routine and schedule of a monastery or convent, it can be hard to find the self-discipline to make prayer part of every action, every day, every season. So you'll need a game plan.

"The first step to bringing prayer into our lives is to *want* to pray. Just as we arc concerned for the health and well-being of ourselves, so we need to take a stance of wanting to pray," Sister Elizabeth told me.

She suggests establishing a "foundation" by reading Scripture and finding a verse or theme or word—*peace, love, breath of God,* or whatever speaks to you—you can repeat or contemplate throughout the day. When you spend time in this mode, it feeds your soul and your desire for deeper prayer, she explains, adding that most critical to a life of prayer is the practice of a morning offering, a surrendering to God each day.

"To breathe each morning, 'What I do today is for *you,*' confirms your dedication. To see God in the present moment is part of the discipline," she says. "Prayer becomes the foundation to my daily existence; it takes me through storms and calm. You and I then can move through life peacefully."

Moving Meditation

Put a small sacred reminder above your bed or next to your alarm clock so as soon as you open your eyes each day, you're prompted to put yourself in God's presence. Or set your alarm clock to wake you up to the sounds of nature, or chant or your favorite spiritual hymn. Be sure the item or song you choose is something that will steer your mind toward goodness and love and away from dread or indifference as you face the challenges of another day.

FOR EVERYTHING THERE IS A SEASON

In his cookbook *This Good Food: French Vegetarian Recipes from a Monastery Kitchen*, Benedictine Brother Victor-Antoine d'Avila-Latourrette not only provides recipes based on seasonal, locally grown foods, as is monastic tradition, but also offers a glimpse into the *ora-et-labora* mind-set of the monastery.

The monk strives for unceasing prayer, he explains, through the hours of silent prayer and a "continual effort to remain conscious of the living God, in whose presence the monk stands."

The same practice can work for you. You may not be living in a cell inside the walls of a monastic enclosure, and you may not have time for hours of silent prayer, but you, too, can be conscious of God always in your presence. It comes back around to the recurring theme of this book: weaving prayer into *everything*, not just sacred things.

"The balance between prayer, sacred reading and manual work—which includes work in the garden and tending the animals—constitutes the life-rhythm of the monastic day," Brother Victor writes in *This Good Food*.

Start to look at the "life-rhythm" of your day. Is it totally out of balance, with most of your time spent running from one stressful moment to another? Or do you have a peaceful "refrain" that keeps the melody of your life from turning dissonant? Actively work toward bringing balance into your daily life by making prayer the thing you constantly come back to for refreshment, rest, and renewal.

Take notice of how life varies from day to day, season to season, year to year. Start to adapt your prayer life and your home life to the seasons, marking time with specific practices that keep your life in tempo with the movement of Mother Earth.

Practical Wisdom

I wonder how long it would take you to notice the regular recurrence of the seasons if you were the first man on earth. What would it be like to live in open-ended time broken only by days and nights?

—Annie Dillard, *Pilgrim at Tinker Creek*

St. Benedict's Rule also states that monks are to welcome all guests as if they are welcoming Christ himself, and so hospitality is a critical part of the mission of any monks and nuns who live by the Rule. That's something that can easily translate to your life, too. Whether you have a big family or live alone, it's inevitable that guests will visit from time to time. Did you ever imagine having friends over could qualify as a spiritual experience? Thanks to St. Benedict, you can take dinner parties to a whole new level, no matter what you're serving or how beautiful your home. Who needs Martha Stewart?

Although on the surface it could appear disjointed—welcome guests, say the Hours, work in the field—the truth is that Benedictine spirituality, and so much of Catholic spirituality in general, is meant to be holistic, with the many different aspects of life coming together in a unified movement that reaches, always, for God.

By taking this monastic approach to everyday life, you can create a sacred rhythm, moving in time with the Spirit, coming back to your own prayer refrain or theme as you care for your family, entertain guests, clean your house, and work in your office. If you begin to recognize that God is in everything and everyone around you, all of life becomes a symphony, with every living thing playing its own melody under the guidance of the master conductor.

Decluttering Your Home and Soul

Lately, I've become obsessed with the clutter around my house—the piles of bills and credit card applications and catalogs that arrive daily in the mail, the mounds of school papers that come home in duplicate and triplicate in backpacks filled to overflowing, the toys crammed into closets, and the clothes so tightly packed into drawers they can't help but come out wrinkled.

The clutter is nothing new, but my recent approach to it is. My new compulsion to rid our lives of excess doesn't have so much to do with cleanliness, as it has to do with godliness. I am convinced that the outward clutter in our house is causing inward clutter in our souls.

Monks and nuns living in monasteries are not surrounded by piles of unopened mail, dusty knickknacks, and boxes of books that haven't been read in a decade. That would be too distracting to the interior work at hand. Instead, they live in mostly bare rooms, called cells, where their attention cannot be diverted by anything unimportant.

Zen design is similar. Anything superfluous is stripped away to leave lots of empty space because empty space and order on the outside leads to empty space and order on the inside—or at least it helps. You can't combat the mental and emotional chaos you're likely to experience in contemplation if you don't first combat the physical chaos in your kitchen or bedroom or wherever it is you spend most of your time.

Less Is More

You can see the trickle-down effect of the chaos conundrum in our modern lives, where our proverbial plates are beyond full—from the literal plate heaped with too much food to the figurative plate heaped with too many commitments and too many possessions. Just look at all the storage unit facilities that have popped up around the country to accommodate America's owning obsession.

We are so uncomfortable with the void of silence and empty space that we'll do anything to fill it with noise and "stuff," even when that stuff isn't necessary—or good for us. Is it any wonder, then, that when we try to clear our minds and make room for God to enter, we find ourselves tripping over so much mental refuse we often give up rather than wade through it?

While you don't have to become an ascetic to pray more deeply, it does help if you can shed some of the unnecessary material belongings and practice a little detachment with regard to the rest of your possessions and relationships.

"Most of us are not called to live a life of intentional abject poverty, especially when we are child raisers and jobholders. We are, however, called as Christians to simplicity and frugality," writes Brian C. Taylor, in his book, *Spirituality for Everyday Living: An Adaptation of the Rule of St. Benedict*. "All of us, if we are to follow the Gospel of Christ, must continually and honestly ask ourselves at what point we are making idols out of what we enjoy, at what point our possessions possess us, just how much is enough."

Notes from the Journey

Until recently, our second car was a 10-year-old sedan covered in dozens of dings and a few small dents on the roof, courtesy of rogue foul balls at the Little League field. Despite the fact that we had a much nicer, more comfortable minivan, I often opted to take the Camry whenever I could. With the minivan, I would feel panic set in every time I pulled into a parking lot dotted with shopping carts, but with the Camry, I'd seek out the closest spot, even if it was also the tiniest, tightest spot in the lot, knowing there was nothing anything could do that could really "hurt" the car.

That's a freeing feeling, one that made me realize how attached I am to my possessions—not because I want more or better things, but because I'm so afraid of losing or damaging what I have.

That might not appear to have anything to do with spirituality, but I'm beginning to realize that holding on so tightly to my possessions and my relationships makes it hard for me to let go with God. I need to become better at seeing my things for what they are—a car to get me to the store, a house to shelter me from rain and cold—and not let those things define me or rule my life.

Stripping Away the Extras

When you think about simplifying your life, you may feel a twinge of fear, thinking you need to get rid of all your beloved possessions. Take heart. You don't have to do that. Yes, starting to unburden yourself of all the unnecessary stuff is good and healthy, but mainly this is about letting go of your attachment to things, even simple, inexpensive things or habits.

In her inspiring book *The Holy Way: Practices for a Simple Life*, Paula Huston writes about her realization that acting on her every desire or wish would not take her where she needed to go. Through small experiments at first, she began to understand how much of her time and energy was spent trying to fulfill those desires.

"My 'wantings,' I discovered, even the most innocent of them, were a constant interruption on my concentration. They pull me away from my writing desk for a handful of almonds. They sent me upstairs in the middle of a serious conversation to change into a warmer pair of socks. They sent waves of self-righteous anger churning through me when a colleague failed to correctly 'read' and then capitulate to, my unexpressed desire to teach the class he'd been assigned," she writes. "Each time a desire arose, I had to mentally deal with it—and this was taking literally hours out of my days."

As she became more aware of her own desires, Huston started noticing those people who made due without, who lived in a "lighter, less encumbered way."

"Not surprisingly, many of these folks could be found in the hermitage: Fr. Bernard with his 'holey' jacket and mismatched sandals; Br. Joshua and the old pickup he's driven for years; Br. Emmanuel, who prays over broken generators. Just as [John] Cassian claimed it would, this lightness in their lives has led to possibilities most people cannot envision," Paula writes, alluding to the first-century monk John Cassian, whose writings influenced St. Benedict.

Think about the last time you had to go on a trip with nothing more than a carry-on bag. Chances are you managed just fine with very few possessions and choices, a couple possible outfits, and none of the extra accessories you have at home. Your daily routine was likely streamlined to a point of total ease.

On vacation, the lack and lightness are seen as good things, so why not try it at home? Lighten your material load in simple ways. Go through your closets, drawers, attic, and basement, and donate anything you haven't worn or used in the past year. Pare down your everyday wardrobe, diet, entertainment choices, and more. You'll feel lighter physically, mentally, and spiritually, and someone else will benefit from your generosity.

Notes from the Journey

One night, after Hurricane Irene wreaked havoc on areas not that far from our home, my husband asked what I would grab—assuming our children were already safe—if I had to leave our house at a moment's notice with only the things I could carry in my arms. After some serious thought, I was happy to realize there was nothing in my house that was so important to me I would absolutely have to take it with me. (Of course, technology makes it easier because things like photos and videos are hanging out in a technological "cloud" somewhere.)

Still, I hope I never have to make that choice, but knowing I don't feel attached to any piece of jewelry or artwork or equipment—not even my guitar or camera—made me feel relieved. Maybe, just maybe, detachment is possible when we set our sights on something bigger and better than anything we can buy or own.

CULTIVATING SILENCE IN A NOISY WORLD

When it comes to creating a life of balance and spiritual health, silence has to be part of the mix, no matter how noisy your everyday life might be. It's only in silence that you can really listen with the "ear of your heart," as St. Benedict taught. But that silence will never happen unless you put in some serious effort. Our world just isn't built for it anymore.

In her book *Listening Below the Noise: A Meditation on the Practice of Silence*, Anne E. LeClaire talks about the fact that people today have become "estranged" from silence.

"Noise is a form of violence done to us, but we have become so accustomed to it that it barely registers, like a car alarm that blares on and on but which no one heeds. Sound systems have become part of our communal landscape, inescapable in supermarkets, shopping malls, ballparks, elevators, coffee shops and restaurants, office waiting rooms and hospitals. It's as if we have come to believe that silence is a void that must be filled whatever the cost," writes LeClaire, whose book chronicles her days of regular silence, long stretches when she does not talk to anyone at all, including her husband when he's right beside her.

"But our spirit has an instinct for silence," she says. "Every soul innately yearns for stillness, for a space, a garden, where we can till, sow, reap, and rest, and by doing so come to a deeper sense of self and our place in the universe. Silence is not an absence but a presence. Not an emptiness but repletion. A filling up."

Begin to develop your "instinct for silence." You'll probably find that you begin to crave silence after you have regular servings of it in your day or week.

Pope Benedict XVI, in his message for the forty-sixth World Communication Day, focused on the need for silence, which is fascinating considering the whole point of the annual message is how to communicate. The pope recognized what many of us choose to ignore: it is only from the deep well of prayerful silence that we find the words and actions to best live out what we believe.

"Silence is an integral element of communication; in its absence, words rich in content cannot exist. In silence, we are better able to listen to and understand ourselves; ideas come to birth and acquire depth; we understand with greater clarity what it is we want to say and what we expect from others; and we choose how to express ourselves," Pope Benedict says. "By remaining silent we allow the other person to speak, to express him or herself; and we avoid being tied simply to our own words and ideas without them being adequately tested. In this way, space is created for mutual listening, and deeper human relationships become possible."

The pope goes on to say that it's often in silence that the most "authentic" communication takes place, through gestures, body language, facial expressions, and more.

"When messages and information are plentiful, silence becomes essential if we are to distinguish what is important from what is insignificant or secondary," he says.

DEALING WITH DISTRACTIONS

Although I work at home and spend a good part of my day completely alone, I'm not necessarily in silence. I keep music playing, talk on the phone, instant message back and forth with my husband via computer, and chatter to myself, along with all the other incidental and inevitable noises I can't control. But recently I decided to expand my daily silent breakfasts into occasional days of deep silence.

On my silent days, I don't listen to music. I don't make phone calls. I don't sign onto Facebook or instant message, and I only check emails once or twice, and only for work purposes. My prayers are totally silent. I even try to refrain from talking to myself and my two cats—something I realize I do throughout the day. From the time my youngest child heads to school around 9 A.M. until my oldest comes home around 2:45 P.M., I am in total silence. It's such a difference from my typically "silent" days I now realize aren't silent at all.

I am incredibly calm and grounded on my silent days, even when things around me are swirling with stress and uncertainty. I find myself saying the Jesus Prayer more frequently, or just staring quietly out a window as I write or sip coffee, not worrying about whether I should also make a phone call or answer an email. On silent days, I'm more inclined to sit down to formal prayer or extend my yoga practice into meditation—something I'm often too "busy" to do on regular days.

In deep silence, I begin to notice how often I fill otherwise empty space with unnecessary talking, emailing, or social networking. So much for my claim I have *no* time for prayer.

Practical Wisdom

When I am liberated by silence, when I am no longer involved in the measurement of life, but in the living of it, I can discover a form of prayer in which there is effectively, no distraction. My whole life becomes a prayer. My whole silence is full of prayer. ... Let me seek then the gift of silence, and poverty, and solitude, where everything I touch is turned into prayer: where the sky is my prayer, the birds are my prayer, the wind in the trees is my prayer, for God is all in all.

—Thomas Merton, *Thoughts in Solitude*

Turn Off, Tune Out

For the next few hours, pay attention to all the noises you hear. Not just the talking from the next cubicle or the voice on the other end of the phone, but the smaller, less-obvious noises—the ding of emails coming in, tweets being posted, texts being sent, Facebook chats being initiated, the melodic tune played by the washer and dryer when they finish a cycle, the rat-a-tat-tat of construction workers, the music on the car radio, the honking horn of the truck behind you. Whatever sounds float your way, make note of them.

How many of those sounds stir a little angst in you, maybe without you even realizing it at first? The email dings, and you worry it's about that project you're struggling with. The phone rings, and you fear one of the kids is calling from the nurse's office.

Now, how many of those sounds can you remove from your life? Some are easy, while others are impossible. But begin to turn off the unnecessary audio tracks of your life.

Sometimes, even in regular silence, I can get distracted, my thoughts running to and fro, my shoulders hunched up to my ears as I write. I recently decided to add a sound to my usual mix of noise in order to bring about more silence. Sounds contradictory, I know, but it works.

I downloaded a "mindfulness bell" and set it to ring at the top of every hour. It sounds like a Himalayan singing bowl being struck just once. As it resonates, I silently pray the Jesus Prayer over and over.

Now, as soon as I hear the first little dull "thunk" that precedes the actual bell, I can feel my shoulders sink away from my ears and the furrow on my forehead smoothes. "Lord Jesus Christ, Son of God, have mercy on me, a sinner," I whisper before I return to my work. Even when I'm not at my desk, I can hear the bell ringing, and I smile to myself and breathe and pray wherever I happen to be. The bell calls me back to my center, to my prayer, and to God.

Moving Meditation

With awareness and mindfulness, even the dinging and honking and beeping around you can become sounds of silence. Choose one of the recurring sounds in your life, one of the noises you can't turn off, and make it a call to prayer. Every time you hear it, stop for a second and breathe deep. Maybe whisper a prayer or a word that calms you. Find that place of silence you crave. Become the silence.

THE WHISPER OF THE SPIRIT

When you're adept at navigating longer periods of silence at home and have added short bursts of silent prayer into your daily routine, you'll find that you're more open to the movement of the Spirit in your life and probably a lot more calm in general. Silence has a way of quieting the nervous energy.

Use your silent periods for some serious prayer. Try your hand at *Lectio Divina*, meditation, or contemplation. Listen with the ear of your heart. If you can devote a solid 20 minutes to silent prayer on a regular, if not daily, basis, you'll begin to see dramatic changes in your prayer life and your perspective.

If that's just too much silence for you at this point, you can make big spiritual strides by simply taking advantage of any silence you can grab—while you're sipping coffee in the morning, while you're in

your car on the highway, while you're cleaning up after dinner. Say
a short prayer to yourself, or just breathe deeply and clear your
heart and head so there's room for God to enter into your space.

Remember the prophet Elijah from the Old Testament? He stood
on a mountain waiting for the Lord to pass by. He expected to find
God in the strong winds, in an earthquake, and in fire, but God
opted for something less flashy:

> After the fire there was a tiny whispering sound.
> When he heard this, Elijah hid his face in his
> cloak and went and stood at the entrance of the
> cave. (1 Kings 19:12)

If you never make time for silent prayer, you just might miss the
still, small voice of the Spirit present amid the figurative storms and
fires that vie for your attention each day.

Everyday Hermits

I once met a Trappist Brother who had lived many years as a hermit
in South America. Brother Leo was talkative and social and devoted
to the poor, so it was hard to understand why he wanted to retreat
from the world, even from the silent world of his regular monastery,
to go to an even more silent and isolated place.

Then again, sometimes when I'm feeling run down and overwhelmed, I imagine how healing it would be to spend some time
in silent solitude. The closest I've ever come to that was a weekend
retreat at the Cistercian Abbey of the Genesee. Although I hadn't
requested it, I was assigned the "hermit room" at the retreat guest
house. At first I was a little disappointed. All the other rooms had
lovely beds with big, thick mattresses; my hermit bed was no more
than what appeared to be a low picnic table topped with a thin mat-
tress. The one plus was the fact that mine was the only room with a
private bathroom. We hermits need our space, you know.

Although I ate meals with the other guests—in silence, of course—and prayed with the monks at the monastery chapel, I was more isolated from the rest of the retreat guests, whose rooms were all clustered together down the hall with a shared bathroom. I set up a small prayer space in my hermit room, with a cross and icon, some Queen Anne's lace I had picked up on a meditative walk, my battery candle, my journal, and my prayer books, and settled into my solitude.

By the end of the retreat, I knew that if I ever return to Genesee, I'll request the hermit room again because I liked the separateness and solitude that were so atypical for me.

Silence provides the perfect entrée into solitude—another practice that's uncommon in modern society and uncomfortable for those used to constant social interaction, either face-to-face or virtual. But it's in solitude that you'll really be able to begin to dig deep down into your thoughts, your beliefs, and your relationship with God.

A PLACE APART

Can you get any regular time alone? I know it's a rarity for those with busy families, full-time jobs, and lots of other commitments, but if you can carve out some alone time now and then—once a year, once a season, once a month—you'll find you're better able to handle the rest of your life.

In her book *Simplify Your Life*, Elaine St. James recommends one day of solitude per month, whether you spend it hiking a mountain, sitting quietly in a park, going to an art museum, spending time alone at home, or a combination of these.

"While it doesn't necessarily mean getting away from people, it definitely means getting away from people you know who are likely to make demands on you," she writes. "Spending time away from the constant barrage of pressures we face can get us back in touch with what is real, and can help to alleviate the tensions of everyday life."

Time in solitude allows for deeper prayer. The monks and nuns of the early Church sought solitude in the desert, where they could pray without ceasing and live simple, often austere, lives.

Find your "desert," a place where you can be totally alone with your thoughts and with God, a place where you won't be tempted to work or do chores or make phone calls or check email. Try to get there regularly, even if it's just once a year for a retreat, something I discuss in more detail in Chapter 9, but preferably more often than that.

YOUR OWN BEST COMPANY

Maybe you already have the time and location for solitude but, frankly, you just don't want to deal with it. Spending time alone can be a scary prospect, especially if you're used to lots of family and friends and co-workers coming in and out of your office, your home, and your life.

What is it that makes you cringe at the thought of spending hours alone and in silence? Is it the fear of facing something you don't want to think about? Is it the fear of being by yourself, with your-self? Start to unravel some of these thoughts. Pray on it. Talk to God. Get to know yourself. The payoff is huge. When you're com-fortable hanging with just your own sweet self, the sky's the limit. Really, think about it. If you can do silence and solitude, you're golden. You can exist anywhere.

Margaret Silf, in her book *Wayfaring: A Gospel Journey in Everyday Life*, addresses the fear that sometimes comes with solitude and isolation, saying it requires a "radical reappraisal" of yourself.

"If we had to give a name to the archenemy of life, we might call it 'fear'—of loneliness, of isolation, of rejection, of emptiness, of meaninglessness and non-existence. Fear makes us into cowards and bullies, doormats and tyrants, perpetrators and colluders in the inherent evils of our system," she writes.

"Our encounter with the darkness within us must leave us humbled yet also with a true sense of wonder," Silf continues. "The wonder is that in all this mayhem, in which reality itself has been utterly distorted and overturned—in ourselves, in our relationships, in all our human society, and in the cosmos itself—in all of this we not only survive, but grow."

Make friends with yourself, and start to discover the wonderful person you are. In silence and solitude, you can get beyond the fear of rejection, the fear of isolation, the fear of meaninglessness, and discover a place of absolute peace, a place where you are loved unconditionally by the God who created you to be exactly who you are right now.

SOLITUDE IN A CROWD

Obviously, anyone living out in the world today can't—or won't—get much time alone. It's just a fact of life. Even if you love being on your own, chances are, life will conspire against you.

Not to worry. When you're an expert at being alone, you can teach yourself to keep that solitary feeling even when you're surrounded by other people. This is not about being antisocial; it's about being pro-serenity.

When you're connected to God through regular prayer and you've developed a regular silent practice, staying calm, quiet, and anchored in your own space will become second nature, even when the world around you is shifting and spinning and tempting you to join the fray.

Every once in a while, you meet someone who has this down pat. You watch from a distance as they maneuver the rocky shoals of social gatherings, office spats, or family tensions without so much as a furrowed brow. It's not magic, and it's not an act. It's the result of real self-knowing, prayer, and a deep connection to the larger universe.

By going inward on a regular basis, you give yourself the strength to keep that peaceful, easy feeling even in the midst of chaos. That silence and solitude will feed your deeper need for self-knowledge and spirituality.

Think back to the life of Jesus. We often see him retreat into the desert by himself for times of deep prayer. And so it should be for you. Wherever your desert is located, whenever you're able, seek time alone—with God and with yourself.

Practical Wisdom

Be still, and know that I am God.
—Psalm 46:10

GOING FORWARD ...

- † Look to the monastics, specifically Benedictine spirituality, as a model of how to weave prayer into the hours of your day-to-day life.
- † By removing the clutter from your home and your life, you remove the spiritual "clutter" in your soul and open a space for deeper prayer.
- † Periods of regular silence can help you learn to listen with the "ear of your heart," as St. Benedict taught.
- † Learning to enjoy solitude can become a pathway to self-acceptance and a deeper relationship with God.
- † Find a "desert" place where you can retreat on occasion to regain your spiritual strength and sanity.

8

DARK NIGHTS AND
DRY SPELLS

If you've been following the advice and suggestions in this book so far, you're probably becoming pretty well-versed in everyday prayer. And right about now you just might be feeling, well, nothing.

One of the most common frustrations with prayer is that it can often feel like an exercise in futility. You won't (usually) get the immediate gratification you get with other efforts. You go on a healthy eating kick, for example, and you see the rewards in pounds lost and energy gained. You take up a running program and watch as your stamina and distance increase day by day.

With prayer, the results are more subtle, if they're noticeable at all, and sometimes it can feel downright empty and dark as you're waiting for a response. It can get so bad you might even want to give up. Don't.

IS ANYBODY OUT THERE?

I wish I could offer you some sort of hard proof that God is standing at the ready, waiting to take your call. Neither I nor anyone else—no matter how soaked in theology and spirituality they may be—can give you any guarantees when it comes to God. That's where the whole faith thing comes in.

But I can tell you this: Catholics believe God is always ready to receive your prayers. Actually, even better than that. The Catholic faith teaches that God is *longing* for your prayers, that he is patiently waiting for you, facing you, desperate for you to realize, finally, that you need him and should reach out to him.

From that perspective, then, it's not God who's MIA; it's the rest of us. God is present at all times and in all things. But that doesn't mean you'll always feel God hovering nearby, and that reality can take its toll.

Feelings of emptiness in your everyday prayer life are modern-day versions of what the sixteenth-century mystic St. John of the Cross called the "dark night of the soul." In every spiritual journey, darkness and emptiness, dryness and abandonment are bound to crop up now and then, sometimes for long stretches. I hate to tell you to expect this, but if you haven't already gotten a taste of the dark night, you really do need to be prepared.

Practical Wisdom

If a man wishes to be sure of the road he treads on, he must close his eyes and walk in the dark.

—St. John of the Cross

How Do I Know God Is Listening?

On a fairly regular basis, I slip into a pit of despair where prayer is concerned. Being a bit of a perfectionist, I figure I must be doing something wrong if I don't get the answers I want on the schedule I'm keeping. I want prayer to move forward on my human terms, forgetting that God's plans may be very different from my own.

Sometimes that seems like reason enough to throw in the towel, but then I remember I'm in good company down in my pit. Many of the saints and holy people throughout the ages have found themselves in this same dark place.

Hanging next to my desk is a quote from Thomas Merton, who provides me with endless comfort because he was so willing to put his human weakness out there for all to see. Whenever I read this reflection, I remember that the spiritual journey can be a difficult one to navigate if I refuse to think outside the (prayer) box:

> MY LORD GOD, I have no idea where I am
> going. I do not see the road ahead of me. I can-
> not know for certain where it will end. Nor do I
> really know myself, and the fact that I think that
> I am following your will does not mean that I am
> actually doing so. But I believe that the desire to
> please you does in fact please you. And I hope I
> have that desire in all that I am doing. I hope that
> I will never do anything apart from that desire.
> And I know that if I do this you will lead me by
> the right road though I may know nothing about
> it. Therefore will I trust you always though I may
> seem to be lost and in the shadow of death. I will
> not fear, for you are ever with me, and you will
> never leave me to face my perils alone.

That just about says it all, doesn't it? You might want to copy that and hang it somewhere obvious so you can remember you're not alone. We're all in this together—the saints and sages before us and everyone around us right now—and our job is to keep moving forward, even when we feel like quitting, even when we wonder if anyone is out there listening to our prayers.

Sometimes we're afraid to admit feeling that way, as if it's a sign of spiritual weakness, or worse, unbelief. It's okay to feel doubt and confusion sometimes, as long as you don't give up on prayer. Just keep praying, even when it feels empty, because it's not. You're just stuck in a dark moment.

When I feel myself slipping into that place, I make my regular prayer this line from the Gospel of Mark: "I do believe, help my unbelief!" (Mark 9:24) It reminds me that I'm not the first to believe with all my heart but feel a shimmer of doubt somewhere deep inside because I can't see the answers to my prayers manifesting themselves in my life in concrete ways.

Moving Meditation

The next time you feel darkness or emptiness seeping into your prayer life, redouble your efforts. Rather than skip your prayer time, try to pray more frequently throughout your day. Change up your routine, perhaps adding in a prayer practice you've never tried before. Pick up a book on prayer or the life of a saint, and read a few pages before bed or during your lunch hour. And all the while, accept the darkness, knowing it will pass if you persevere.

MY PRAYERS AREN'T WORKING

Typically I go to God with a laundry list of things I need, but sometimes I'm so mentally and spiritually exhausted I just sit there, pleading, *What? What? WHAT?!?!?* I keep waiting for a sign, an answer, something to let me know the words I'm saying aren't getting lost in translation. It's rare that God comes back with a nice, neat, and direct answer, but every once in a while, usually when I'm least expecting it, there it is.

Not long ago, I was in a bad spiritual place. Due to a confluence of events, I found myself wondering if perhaps I'd said all I had to say, in terms of my Catholic writing. I was thinking maybe it was time to hang it up. As I pondered this, I prayed. I asked God for some sort of sign that my writing wasn't in vain. I even emailed one friend asking for prayers and telling her how much I wished God could write me a letter, spelling everything out in black and white so there would be no mistaking his message. That was on a Wednesday.

Fast-forward to Friday. A letter arrived from a religious sister I once worked with at my first job. I haven't seen or heard from this sister in about 25 years. She keeps up with my life through my "Life Lines" column, which runs in her diocesan newspaper. Here's a snippet of what Sister Michaelita wrote: "Your efforts to lead a prayerful life amidst all your responsibilities and the demands that are made upon your time have truly impressed and encouraged me."

I "encouraged" her? I was somewhat stunned but so happy to hear from this long-lost person from my past. I didn't think anything more of it, beyond deciding to send her a copy of one of my books. I certainly didn't make a connection to my letter request.

On Saturday, I opened the mailbox and found a card from a fellow Catholic blogger, someone known for her knack for personal note-writing, but still, today? Right now? Fran thanked me for all I do and for my life "as a sign of Christ." Wow. The card included a quote from St. Francis de Sales (one of my all-time favorites) about entering into silence (one of my most recent quests). Perfect.

I still wasn't catching on ….

No mail Sunday but then came Monday. Two—count 'em—two personal letters arrived. One was a note from my friend Maureen, which, among other things, offered encouragement as I embarked on a big writing project. The other was from Brother Christian, a Trappist monk I met on retreat the month before. "See Jesus and Mary everywhere and adore their wills lovingly, and you will be a saint," he wrote, in a handwritten card that also included a page from a book on St. Therese.

Now I was getting suspicious. I had prayed for a sign, I had wished for a letter, and suddenly letters were coming every day. And not just any letters. Letters that offered encouragement, prayers, friendship, and inspiration. Suddenly I was overwhelmed by what God was doing for me in the most obvious and concrete ways.

I thought that would be the end of it, but Tuesday came and the phone rang. I almost didn't pick it up because I didn't recognize the name, but I did anyway. The woman on the other end had gone on a retreat with me several years ago. We see each other once in a while after Mass, but she had never called my house before. I couldn't imagine what she might want or need.

She called, she said, to let me know how much she enjoys and appreciates my work and to apologize for not getting to a recent talk I gave at my parish. That call was really the icing on the cake. I felt humbled by the embarrassment of prayer riches God was showering down on me. All I could do was say thank you, thank you, thank you, and hope I'd remember this moment when some dark shadow casts a pall over my spiritual landscape down the road, which, let's face it, is only inevitable.

God does not typically answer my prayers in such obvious fashion. Normally I'm searching, listening, hoping for some little shred of something to indicate my message was received. Unfortunately, that's the norm for most people, even the saints.

Blessed Mother Teresa of Calcutta's dark night lasted for years and years, unknown to the outside world until after her death when her letters were published. Throughout the spiritual darkness, she continued her mission and ministries, she continued to spread the Gospel through her words and actions, and she continued to pray, but she didn't necessarily feel anything in return.

"In January 1955, a little less than a year since she had last mentioned the darkness to Archbishop Perier, Mother Teresa noted a new element in her experience: deep loneliness. This loneliness, her 'travel companion' from this point forward, resulted from her apparent separation from God and those she trusted most. This sense of alienation made her cross harder to bear," writes Missionary of Charity Father Brian Kolodiejchuk in his commentary on Mother Teresa's letters.

Mother Teresa, in one of her letters to the archbishop, writes: "there is such a deep loneliness in my heart I cannot express it … How long will our Lord stay away?"

If Mother Teresa—a woman seen by the world as a living saint during her lifetime and now on the official road to canonization—can have such deep, dark loneliness in her prayer life, why should you or I assume we can avoid it, even in much smaller doses? Try to take comfort in the knowledge that others have been there and continued the journey in spite of it, or in the midst of it.

When you don't feel like your prayers are working, lay it all on the line before God. Tell God your struggles. Get mad if you need to; he can take it. If you have a spiritual friend, a spiritual director, or someone else you can talk to, share your feelings and soak up any insights. Often it's hard to see the answers right in front of you because you're so wrapped up in expecting specific things, answers of your own making.

LOOKING BEYOND ANSWERS

Part of the problem with prayer often lies in the fact that we expect any answers at all. Prayer is not a fast-track to getting what we want, as you probably know all too well at this point. Prayer is meant to be a pathway to union with Jesus Christ, a means of attaining eternal life one small step at a time.

When you begin to weave prayer into everyday life, prayer becomes less of a spiritual bartering system and more of an overall way of life. By praying every day and throughout the day, you get away from prayer as something you have to do, a hoop you must jump through to get what you want, and begin to see it as the thing that keeps you heading in the right direction, no matter what's happening in the rest of your life.

Practical Wisdom
___
When we pray to God we must be seeking nothing—nothing.
—Saint Francis of Assisi
___

LEARNING TO ACCEPT A NONANSWER

Even with this clear understanding of prayer, you'll still go to God with specific requests—for yourself and others. That's not going to change. The difference will come in how you deal with the answers you get, the answers you don't want, and the answers that never seem to arrive.

When my mother was dying of cancer 24 years ago, I prayed desperately for a miracle. I was convinced my prayers would be answered because my earlier prayers for my grandmother, who'd been hit by a car while crossing a street, seemed to fall on deaf ears. Surely I wouldn't strike out twice.

My maternal grandfather was on his own quest for a miracle. A devout Catholic who attended at least two Masses a day and spent hours praying in silence in front of the Blessed Sacrament, he began saying the Divine Mercy Novena for my mother. But having a deeper understanding of prayer than I did at the time, he prayed that God's will be done, not his own.

When my mother went rapidly downhill and died a few days later, most of my family was in shock. How did this happen? Where was God? I was in a spiritual rage that verged on utter hopelessness and doubt. My grandfather, on the other hand, stood by stoically, insisting that God *did* answer our prayers, just not the way we wanted or expected. In his mind, the fact that his daughter did not have to suffer for weeks or months was an answer unto itself.

It's not easy to let go of the answers we want. So often it's only in hindsight that we can figure out how the answer we dreaded led us to where we needed to be. So part of this prayer journey is not just about learning to pray but about learning to let go of what we expect in return. Pray simply because you want to love God more deeply, grow closer to Jesus, and eventually be united with him in heaven.

As they sang in the 1970s Broadway hit *Godspell*, "Day by day, day by day, oh, dear Lord, three things I pray, to see thee more clearly, love thee more dearly, follow thee more nearly, day by day." Whether you sing it or say it, that's the general gist of what prayer is meant to "accomplish."

TRUST AND SURRENDER

Jesuit Father Walter Ciszek was captured by the Russian army during World War II, convicted as a "Vatican spy," and forced to serve 23 brutal years in Soviet prisons and in the labor camps of Siberia. In his powerfully moving book *He Leadeth Me*, Father Ciszek chronicles his years in captivity—the torture, the horror, the threats of execution, but especially the faith that kept him going. At one point, when he reached a point of complete spiritual blackness, he realized a kind of fear and trembling that not even the worst Soviet punishments could produce in him.

"This was despair. For that one moment of blackness, I had lost not only hope but the last shreds of faith in God. I had stood alone in a void and I had not even thought of or recalled the one thing that had been my constant guide, my only source of consolation in all other failures, my ultimate recourse: I had lost the sight of God," he writes, saying that as soon as he recognized this horrible reality, he turned to prayer in an effort to seek the God he had forgotten. There he found consolation—and a moment of conversion.

He realized that God was asking for his absolute trust, a "complete gift of self," and faith that everything was in God's hands.

"Across that threshold I had been afraid to cross, things suddenly seemed so very simple," Father Ciszek writes. "God is in all things, sustains all things, directs all things. To discern this in every situation and circumstance, to see his will in all things, was to accept each circumstance and situation and let oneself be borne along in perfect confidence and trust. Nothing could separate me from him, because he was in all things. No danger could threaten me, no fear could shake me, except the fear of losing sight of him."

Trust and surrender can be especially difficult to embrace when you're in a dark, even scary place. And although you're not likely to find yourself in a situation as difficult as Father Ciszek's—thank goodness—you can take one key truth from his life and his own crisis of faith: the only thing worse than feeling empty and dark and alone is losing sight of God.

So keep coming back to prayer, even when it seems illogical, even when it seems useless, even when it seems empty, even when it's the last thing you want to do. Come back anyway, and place yourself completely in God's hands. Let go of the desire to be the one in control, and surrender to God's will. And if you find yourself falling back into a dark place, pray some more.

Practical Wisdom

Each time we shift from the foot of mastery to the foot of risk it takes a leap of faith, a little gasp in the unknown where God can enter.

—Dawna Markova, *I Will Not Die an Unlived Life*

LEARNING TO PERSEVERE

Renowned theologian Father Henri Nouwen wrote about his own spiritual struggles with remarkable honesty. "Do I like to pray? Do I want to pray? Do I spend time praying? Frankly, the answer is no to all three questions. After sixty-three years of life and thirty-eight years of priesthood, my prayer seems as dead as a rock," he wrote in *Sabbatical Journey*.

He goes on to talk about the tremendous consolation he found in prayer when he was a teenager, when he was discerning his calling to the priesthood, when prayer was "so intimate and so satisfying." But at the time of his writing, he was feeling nothing, he said, describing his prayer life as dark and dry.

Rather than lose faith, however, he united his suffering with Jesus, remembering how Jesus called out from the cross, "My God, my God, why have you forsaken me?" (Matthew 27:46)

"Are the darkness and dryness of my prayer signs of God's absence, or are they signs of a presence deeper and wider than my sense can contain? Is the death of my prayer the end of my intimacy with God or the beginning of a new communion, beyond words, emotions, and bodily sensations?" Nouwen writes. "As I sit down for half an hour to be in the presence of God and to pray, not much is happening …. Still, maybe this time is a way of dying with Jesus."

GETTING BACK UP

Coming back to prayer again and again, even when we don't feel particularly prayerful, requires a pretty big measure of perseverance. People may offer helpful advice, and friends may try to push you along, but when it comes down to it, it's between you and God.

"We have all heard it when we are struggling with an issue. Well-meaning and the not-so-well-meaning people will tell you that 'It is always darkest before the dawn.' It rolls off their tongue without thought, almost as if they are privy to some secret knowledge of your future," writes Karen Anne Mahoney in a post about spiritual darkness on her blog, Write 2 the Point, saying she'd grown weary of people tossing that phrase around as she dealt with so many dark and painful days.

Karen recently decided to have what she calls a "spiritual garage sale," putting her worries about things beyond her control, her regrets, her emotional pain and anger in spiritual boxes on the tag sale table of her life, knowing Jesus would gladly pick up her un-needed and unwanted items.

"Jesus, who so freely gave his life for my sinfulness, is ready to take it all—every box, every bag, every encumbrance, and remove it from my life. All I have to do is ask," says Karen, a wife, mother, and Catholic author living in Wisconsin. Her perspective on life and prayer is changing, she says, adding that although she lost "nearly everything," she is starting to realize just how blessed she is.

"Light abounds—there is no darkness. We may feel dark, but if we carry the light of Jesus within us, no darkness can overcome us. It is his light that offers my freedom, and increases my sense of gratitude for each new day," she says.

Seeing Beyond "Failures"

What could you put out for the taking at your spiritual garage sale? What's keeping you from coming to God in prayer? What resentments and anger, pain and unhappiness are wearying you spiritually? Turn them over to God, and begin to look for the blessings. Gratitude will make you stronger and better able to withstand the tough times.

Like Fathers Merton and Ciszek, like Mother Teresa, like John of the Cross, like so many others, can you begin to look for whatever tiny light there might be in the darkness? Can you embrace the darkness perhaps as the path you are meant to be on in order to reach Jesus Christ?

It's a tall order, I know, but when you begin to look at the darkness and dryness not as a roadblock but as a necessary detour on the spiritual journey, you just might find that your greatest growth comes not when you're full of joy and light and sureness, but when you're faced with sorrow and darkness and doubt.

Notes from the Journey

Lent is my favorite season in the Church year, always has been. The problem is that I often expect too much of Lent, or maybe of myself. But this Lent was different, and not in a good way. Some issues in my personal life—physical problems, mental stress, overwhelming responsibilities—converged to drive me into darkness, a darkness like none I'd known before, or at least none I remember up to this point.

I tried to pray. Nothing. I went to church. Nothing. Holy Week came and even the Mass of the Last Supper didn't move me. I walked up to Communion, hoping upon hope it would pull me out of this dark place. Even on Easter with flowers and holy water and Alleluias filling the church, I felt nothing. A priest friend asked me how my Easter was, and I responded, "Empty and meaningless." I wasn't being melodramatic; I was being brutally honest. And this lasted for a while, even as I wrote parts of this book.

Until I started this chapter, that is. And then, as I plumbed the depths of the dark night and read, read, read what others had to say about spiritual darkness, I felt a little light come on. First it was like the tiniest candle burning way off in the distance. But slowly it got closer and bigger, and as I sat down to pray the next morning, there it was. Nothing major, but something. And just like that, in an instant, my weeks of darkness started to lift.

Becoming a Fool for God

"We are fools on Christ's account," St. Paul writes in his First Letter to the Corinthians. (1 Corinthians 4:10) You probably don't like to think of yourself as a fool, and yet that's what you are called to be, but not in the usual sense. When St. Paul and others who came after him, namely St. Francis of Assisi, used this term, they meant it as something supremely positive although difficult to live.

Being a "fool" for Jesus Christ and for your faith means being willing to step outside society's conventions and live in a way that's true to your calling as a child of God and not a child of the world. As you know, conventional society and Christian faith don't always see eye to eye. Hence, the challenge of being a fool.

Turning the World Upside Down

You may remember from Chapter 1 that I talked about becoming "counter cultural" in the sense that your everyday prayer life and quest for mindfulness run in opposition to the way the world works. Being a fool for Christ is the flip side of the same coin. It is the willingness to go against the grain, even when it's uncomfortable or downright painful.

You don't have to go to St. Francis levels of foolishness—we're talking about a guy who stripped naked in the town square to renounce the ways of the world and live the Gospel more fully. In fact, I beg you *not* to take the St. Francis approach.

So how does being a fool for Christ work in our modern-day world where disrobing in public is frowned upon?

It's often much more subtle than anything you hear about in the saintly stories of history. When you think of the famous fools, you might wonder how this could possibly apply to your life. Someone like St. Maximilian Kolbe, who volunteered to die so a stranger might be saved in the concentration camp at Auschwitz, or St. Kateri Tekakwitha, who had to flee her Mohawk homeland in upstate New York due to persecution brought by her conversion to Christianity, or Blessed Pope John Paul II, who forgave and embraced the man who tried to assassinate him. All these holy people—and too many more to count—displayed a certain foolishness for Christ, a willingness to put their own well-being, their own comfort, their own feelings aside in order to live out the Gospel teachings.

The last of the Beatitudes says, "Blessed are you when people hate you, and when they exclude and insult you, and denounce your name as evil on account of the Son of Man. Rejoice and leap for joy on that day! Behold, your reward will be great in heaven. For their ancestors treated the prophets in the same way." (Luke 6:22–23)

You don't need to go out looking for persecution, but it may show up in your life in not-so-obvious ways, ways that might not even seem like "persecution," but are, in reality, forms of it—when you go to a child's birthday party and another parent lambastes you for your Catholic beliefs (happened to my husband); the days you stand in the rain beside the parish "peace pole" to pray for an end to violence in the world and people drive by shaking their heads; the times you bless yourself and pray before dinner in a restaurant and the people around you shift uncomfortably trying to avert their eyes. It might not seem like persecution as we typically understand it, but it is, and it certainly earns you your stripes as a fool for Christ.

Practical Wisdom

Cheerfulness strengthens the heart and makes us persevere in a good life. Therefore the servant of God ought always to be in good spirits.

—Saint Philip Neri

I gave a retreat day for some catechists in Rhode Island last year, and at the end of the first session, I asked them to write themselves a letter *from* Jesus. I wanted them to see themselves with the eyes of unconditional love. So often we see only our flaws and brokenness, but if we can look at ourselves as God would look at us, we'd see something totally different, something completely beautiful, flaws and all.

The exercise was so well received I wrote a column about it, only to find out later that an online group of atheists had found my column and was mocking me and calling me all sorts of terrible (unprintable) names because of what they perceived to be my foolishness. They couldn't understand how or why someone would do such a thing, and the best they could do was offer cruel, often crude, commentary about me and everything I believe in.

I opted not to read past the first few comments, and although I mostly brushed it off, a part of me was hurt and angry. I know this comes with the territory, especially in light of the fact that I put my beliefs out there in print for the world to see, but sometimes it's still hard to be on the receiving end of such jeers.

DEVELOPING A NEW ATTITUDE

Don't let any of this talk of darkness and dryness and foolishness scare you off. As with any practice, there will be bumps and twists in the road. Prayer will help you manage those, and before you know it, you'll be able to face challenges with a peacefulness you once only dreamed about.

Everyday prayer and spirituality require an internal shift, away from what the world says you should do, be, own, and want, and toward what God calls you to do, be, own, and want. They are often very different things, and through prayer, you'll begin to be able to decipher which is which and how to get to where you're supposed to be, even when it's dark, and even when people think you're crazy for trying.

If you've ever met someone who has reached a point of serious spiritual depth, you've probably marveled at their ability to face the worst trials with trust and maybe even a smile. These are the people who seem to get stronger and surer every time the world knocks them down. They weren't just born that way; they grew into that place of peaceful acceptance and joy through prayer. And it's yours for the taking. All you need to do is stay the course and pray in the everyday.

Practical Wisdom

In daily life we must see that it is not happiness that makes us grateful, but gratefulness that makes us happy.

—Benedictine Brother David Steindl-Rast, theologian and author

GOING FORWARD …

† Sometimes you may wonder if God is listening. Imagine God facing you, waiting for you to come to him in prayer. It's your move.

† Part of spiritual growth is learning to accept the answers God sends, not just the answers you want.

† Prayer is not a barter system, but rather a pathway to union with Jesus Christ.

† Into every spiritual life some darkness and dryness must fall. Remember you are not alone, and persevere in your prayer, even when it feels empty.

† Your quest for holiness may not always be well received by the world around you. Becoming a "fool for Christ" is often part of the territory, as it was for many of the great saints.

9

PILGRIMAGE OF THE HEART

In much the same way a vacation can jump-start your personal life, providing you with renewed energy, interesting experiences, and maybe even creative ideas or new directions for the future, a pilgrimage can jump-start your spiritual life. When you visit sacred sites from a faith perspective, walking in the footsteps of so many spiritual seekers who have gone before you, it changes you inside and out.

Although to the casual observer a pilgrimage may appear to be nothing more than one more trip to an exotic locale or historic building, it's anything but—if it's done right. A pilgrimage requires a mind-set different from the one you might take with you to the beach or a ski resort or a European villa.

When I went to Rome a few years ago, I quickly realized my pilgrimage could deteriorate into an art history tour, as I checked off must-see churches where Caravaggio, Michelangelo, and Bernini masterpieces resided. Caught up in the throngs of regular tourists following their leader's brightly colored flag bobbing above their heads, it would have been easy to cross over from pilgrimage to vacation mind-set.

Even when I walked into St. Peter's Basilica for the first time, the tourist perspective threatened to overwhelm the spiritual one, and I was disappointed. Seems impossible, right? How could a visit to the center of Catholicism, in a basilica filled with sacred awe and historic artworks, be anything less than transcendent?

I was crushed shoulder to shoulder with thousands of other travelers and told I had about 30 minutes inside before I had to meet my group out at the obelisk in the square. I couldn't get near the *Pieta*. I couldn't touch the foot of the St. Peter statue, as millions of pilgrims have done before me, wearing down the toe of the statue to almost nothing. I couldn't kneel before the tombs of popes and saints to pray. I left somewhat let down by what I had hoped would be the pinnacle of my pilgrimage experience. I wanted a do-over.

The next morning at 7 A.M., I returned to St. Peter's with a friend. This time we were the only ones going through security. Once inside, we had the entire basilica mostly to ourselves. In each of the more than 40 chapels lining the sides of the basilica, priests—many of them tourists themselves—were celebrating Mass in their native languages.

This was the experience I had longed for, one where I could feel my faith alive in the familiar refrains of the Mass, even in unfamiliar languages. I attended Mass celebrated in Italian by a Nigerian priest, who gave a few lines of his homily in English when he realized his only two congregants were from the United States. Afterward, I was allowed into a roped-off area to go to confession, cementing the St. Peter's experience in my pilgrim heart. Suddenly, Michelangelo's dome felt as familiar as my own parish church.

For the rest of my trip, I used my many visits to famous churches and off-the-beaten-path chapels to pray for the special intentions I had brought with me at the request of family, friends, blog readers, Facebook friends, and even total strangers I met on a bus. I prayed for all the mothers I know as I knelt before the tomb of St. Monica, whose desperate prayers for her once-wayward son, Augustine, are well known in Catholic history. I lit a candle for a Jesuit priest I know as I knelt before the relics of St. Ignatius, founder of the Society of Jesus. As I went from place to place, I prayed for people I know who were sick and for loved ones who have died, making every stop another leg of my pilgrim journey.

Practical Wisdom

We see in these swift and skillful travelers a symbol of our life, which seeks to be a pilgrimage and a passage on this earth for the way of heaven.

—Pope Paul VI

WALKING THE WAY OF FAITH

A true pilgrimage, in the deepest sense, doesn't require any physical travel at all. It's as much an interior journey as a geographical one. Life itself is a pilgrimage; your ultimate journey is not to a specific shrine but to the core of your being, to that destination in your heart where God resides. No passport or suitcase required.

In the movie *The Way*, the main character, played by Martin Sheen, travels to France to pick up the remains of his son, who died in a tragic accident while walking the famed *Camino de Santiago de Compostela* (the Way of St. James), an 800-kilometer trail through France and Spain that traces the path of the apostle to its end in northwest Spain. For more than 1,000 years, pilgrims have been walking this route, known as the *Camino*, in an effort to gain spiritual insights.

Sheen's character, not a spiritual fellow, decides to finish the walk his son began, and over the miles, you begin to see the impact the pilgrimage has on him in ways he could not predict. Although he covers a great physical distance, it's the spiritual journey that requires him to travel the farthest—to unknown and difficult places inside his heart and soul. As one of the characters explains in the film, no one walks the Way by accident. That's true of the interior journey as well.

Where are you on your pilgrim journey? Are you ready for a "real" pilgrimage, one that may take you places you never intended but were always meant to go? Perhaps an actual, physical pilgrimage might be just the thing to bring new depth and new insights to your everyday prayer life, whether you board a plane and fly to Spain or walk around the corner to a historic church in your own neighborhood.

Although the tradition of pilgrimage dates to our Jewish ancestors and even to the ancient Greeks, Egyptians, and Aztecs, the Christian version of this tradition has its roots in the life of the Holy Family. Mary, Joseph, and Jesus made an annual pilgrimage to Jerusalem. Jesus was crucified during a time of pilgrimage, in fact. Early Christians made pilgrim journeys to the tombs of martyrs, and later Christians went back to the Holy Land. We are a pilgrim people.

"To go on pilgrimage is not simply to visit a place to admire its treasures of nature, art or history," said Pope Benedict XVI during a 2010 trip to Santiago de Compostela. "To go on pilgrimage really means to step out of ourselves in order to encounter God where he has revealed himself, where his grace has shone with particular splendor and produced rich fruits of conversion and holiness among those who believe."

Moving Meditation

Find one sacred place you'd like to visit sometime in the future, and begin doing a little research. If it's a long-term goal, like going to Assisi or the Holy Land, research the history and spirituality of the place or the saint associated with it. Make your preparations for the pilgrimage part of the journey. By the time you make the trip, you'll feel as though you already have an intimate connection to the place. I have a favorite book on St. Francis of Assisi. I take it out every once in a while and read a favorite bookmarked page just to remind myself that someday I will walk those streets, pray in that chapel, and see what Francis saw.

Physical Journeys on the Spiritual Path

Before watching *The Way*, I'd never had much of an urge to walk the *Camino*, but I came away from that movie with a new appreciation for the courage and determination of those people who undertake this level of pilgrimage. It's not for the faint of heart. I know two people who have made this journey, and in the back of my mind, I wonder if perhaps someday I, too, will walk the *Camino*, either on my own, with my husband, or with one of our children.

Even seeing the rigorous terrain, the often-crowded sleeping conditions, and the many difficulties of the *Camino* was not enough to make me cross the possibility off my list of potential pilgrim journeys. Quite the contrary.

Seeing the film reminded me that pilgrimage is about leaving our comfort zones. Yes, physical comfort zones but also spiritual comfort zones. Pilgrimage—as we see through the central characters of *The Way*—is about looking at things we want to ignore, seeing in others what we've never seen before, exploring uncharted territory in our own hearts, healing our brokenness, and finding our truth.

DISTANT LANDS

If you have the ability and opportunity to make a pilgrimage to any one of the many great Catholic holy places around the world—the Holy Land, Rome, Assisi, Lourdes—do it, but be sure to allow yourself enough time to focus on spiritual experiences, not just your tourist itinerary. Oftentimes, the best moments happen in the most unlikely places.

One of the most powerful experiences during my Italy trip occurred on a Friday night near the end of my visit. I ventured over to Santa Maria in Trastevere, one of the oldest churches in Christendom, for its sung vespers service. In this beautiful church filled with stunning icons, I attempted to sing the prayers in Italian, as some young men in the pew with me pointed to the pages and phrases so I could follow along. In the crowded church lit only by flickering candles, tears streamed down my face as I felt the power of faith moving among the people, despite cultural differences, despite language barriers, despite all the things that typically make us strangers to each other. At that moment, we were one.

If you do go on an overseas pilgrimage, do your homework. Research in books and via online sources, but also talk to others who have been there. When you arrive, talk to locals. They'll have the inside scoop on when churches will be less crowded, on what services are best for visitors, and other tips the guidebooks might miss. Be willing to stray from your plans; try to enter into the local community's celebrations rather than watching from the outside. It can make the difference between going home with nothing more than a few nice photos and going home with a sense of spiritual renewal.

> ### Notes from the Journey
>
> My trip to the Roman Forum went horribly off course when I took a wrong turn and walked up a very steep hill in scorching heat only to come to what by all appearances was a dead end. I stood there, lost, sweating, and somewhat frustrated.
>
> But around the bend, I could see a small stucco church, which should have been closed because it was the daily downtime when everyone closes up shop for lunch and a siesta. I pushed on the door, and it opened into a dark and cool church, empty but for one other person and the haunting sound of a lone voice singing a Gregorian chant from somewhere behind the altar.
>
> I sat in the pew and listened and prayed and gave thanks for the unexpected twist, the "mistake," that took me exactly where I needed to be.

CLOSER TO HOME

It's easy to get overwhelmed by the prospect of a pilgrimage to a distant land, but you have plenty of opportunities to become a pilgrim without ever leaving the confines of your own diocese, state, or country.

For 8 years, I lived within a 40-minute drive of the National Shrine of the North American Martyrs in Auriesville, New York, where St. Kateri Tekakwitha was born and where Jesuit missionaries St. Isaac Jogues and St. Rene Goupil and lay missioner St. John Lalande were martyred. It took my son's Boy Scout retreat to get me to make the short trek to the grounds of this beautiful place overlooking the Mohawk Valley.

As I walked that holy ground, praying with other pilgrims, sleeping in a tent not far from the ravine where Rene Goupil died for the faith, I felt immersed in the sacred, as if I were breathing in God's grace with every step, every breath.

A pilgrimage allows you to step outside your routine so you can experience what life can be like when you drop some of your barriers and let God and other people into your heart in new and sometimes scary ways.

One of the most distinct moments of a recent silent retreat came when I was sitting on the deck of the retreat house, reading a book on prayer and writing in a spiritual journal as I watched the sun go down. An older man sat at the other end of the picnic table, sobbing desperately. I didn't know him. I wasn't supposed to talk to him, and yet I ached for him. And I felt love for him, this stranger whose only connection to me was the fact that he'd picked the same retreat center on the same weekend.

So I did the only thing I could do in that moment —I prayed for him. I poured out all my love through prayer and asked God to hear this man's desperate cries, for Mary to hold him in her spiritual arms and give him the comfort he needed. I'd like to say I'd have that same reaction to any other stranger who passed my way back in my "normal" life, but I know I am too busy, too guarded, too cynical to react that way all the time.

A pilgrimage takes you out of that guarded place, and when it drops you back into normal life, you are changed forever. Even if it's only a little bit at first. You come home and, without even realizing it, something has shifted. You may feel you've lost your pilgrim mojo as you navigate the busyness of daily life, but it's still there, in the background, coloring how you react, how you speak, how you pray. Little by little, as you venture out into more pilgrim experiences near and far, you bring that pilgrim spirit to the everyday. Before you know it, even a trip to the store can be a pilgrimage, one where you see Christ in others with love in your heart and joy in your soul.

If you're unable to travel even short distances, you don't have to miss out on the journey. We are all called to be pilgrims; we are all walking a path toward God. Some may walk hundreds of miles along Santiago de Compostela or wade into the waters at Lourdes, but many more will make pilgrim journeys right next door.

Kathryn Jean Lopez, a writer, blogger, and editor-at-large of National Review Online, told me that sometimes pilgrimage is as simple as looking within your daily routine for a hidden oasis of peace in a desert of chaos.

"I am spoiled because I spend most of my time in New York and Washington, both of which [have] some terrific spots for disappearing from the noise, adoring our Lord, asking him to help you with your priorities," she said, giving as examples the Basilica of the National Shrine of the Immaculate Conception on the grounds of The Catholic University in Washington, D.C., and the nearby Franciscan monastery, which she called "a little piece of the Holy Land in America." In Manhattan, she frequents St. Vincent Ferrer Church on 65th Street and Lexington Avenue, Our Saviour Church in the shadow of Grand Central Station, and of course, St. Patrick's Cathedral.

"Sometimes we need to be reminded that it's not just the get-away retreats that are crucial, but the daily ones, too—for the busy executive, for the blue-collar worker, for the busy mom," she said.

Moving Meditation

Find one church, shrine, or other spiritual location within your community or region, and make plans to visit. See if any special celebrations are coming up soon, and try to time your pilgrimage accordingly. Don't fill your trip with a long list of things you need to accomplish. Just go and soak up the sacredness of the place. Sit, kneel, or walk in quiet prayer. If possible, take along some prayer intentions from family and friends and make them part of your journey. Bring some little token of your visit back with you, whether it's a pinecone found on a walk or a purchased item from a gift shop. Add it to your sacred space at home to remind you of the journey you're on.

REGULAR RETREATS

I find I crave slowness and silence more with each passing year. And although I work at home and get a heavy dose of silence on a regular basis, it's not the kind of silence that heals the soul and leaves me refreshed for whatever life throws my way. It helps, for sure, but healing silence comes only through extended periods of quiet and solitude.

Enter the retreat experience, preferably silent or mostly silent. Retreats are something few people get to experience nowadays, but they are so worth the time it takes to drive to the monastery or retreat center. Because no matter how silent you may try to be at home now and then, nothing can prepare you for the deep but difficult work of real inner silence and solitude.

This is where you confront yourself and the things you may try to hide from amid the noise of your daily life. With no iPods or social networking, no televisions or telephones, you come face to face with your true self. If you really make good use of your retreat time through prayer, you come face to face with God.

From what I've experienced on retreat, I think of it as a kind of spiritual detox. First there's denial, as in, *Why am I even here? I should go home and do the laundry and clean the bathrooms.* Then the anger phase: *What's the point? I don't hear God. I don't think my prayers are working.*

With each passing hour, however, things begin to shift. Walls go down, and emotions surface. I begin to recognize how much I fear real silence and how easy it is to drown out the Spirit. It's not unusual, on silent retreat, to see people crying, apparently for no reason at all. Except when you're on retreat, especially a silent retreat, you know very well there's a reason, or many reasons. By the time I leave, I'm clinging to every last second of silence, already looking forward to the next time I can come back to a place that's so elusive, no matter how hard I try to re-create it at home.

When I returned from my last retreat, my teenage son, who only days before was complaining about the sudden silent lull in family conversation, asked if he could come with me the next time I head to the Trappist abbey. Silence speaks volumes, it seems. It echoes in your words and actions, long after you've left it behind. Its scent lingers on you, giving others a taste of what's possible when you listen, as St. Benedict taught, with the "ear of your heart."

Choosing a Retreat

If you've never been on a retreat, or you haven't been on one in a long time, it can be intimidating to make the first move. Where do you go? What kind of retreat do you choose? Do you go alone, with a friend, or as part of a group? It's really up to you and whatever you're hungry for at this point in your spiritual life. If you're going on your first retreat, you may want to attend one that will include conferences, guided prayer, and maybe even some group discussion and sharing. If you're ready for more intense prayer, seek out silent retreats, perhaps directed at first and eventually entirely on your own in a monastery setting.

Knowing a few simple terms helps narrow down your choices:

A *preached* or conference-style retreat is typically for groups. Preached retreats tend to focus on a particular theme—women's spirituality, prayer, or Scripture, for example—with a retreat leader (or team of leaders) presenting talks followed by periods of prayer.

A *guided* retreat is geared toward smaller groups and provides daily conferences and extended time for individual prayer. A spiritual director is typically available for one-on-one consultation.

A *directed* retreat allows you to create your own prayerful retreat within the context of a monastery or retreat center setting. Typically, you meet daily with a spiritual director to discuss concerns and goals.

A *private* or individual retreat is more of a free-form retreat, where you set the parameters. There's no leader or director. A private retreat may be strictly spiritual, or it may be a combination of prayer and restorative activities like drawing and writing, walking, and reading.

Once you've chosen a retreat, knowing a few basic guidelines can help you make the most of the experience. As difficult as it may be for you to disconnect from the world, turn off your cell phone when you arrive at the monastery or retreat center and leave behind all the high-tech gadgets that are likely to distract you. Instead, bring some spiritual reading, but don't get overly ambitious by bringing things that will simply fill up the time meant for prayer.

You should also bring a notebook for jotting down any thoughts about conferences, recommendations from your spiritual director, and personal reflections. Retreat time is perfect for spiritual journaling. And if you're so inclined, bring a few small items from home to create a sacred space in your retreat room. That little display of familiar prayer prompts can make even the most sparse and humble "cell" feel like a spiritual paradise.

Set some specific goals or resolutions for your retreat, but don't be unrealistic or too general. For example, don't just say you'll pray every day; say you'll pray the Liturgy of the Hours each morning, or whatever your goal may be—reading the Gospel, sitting in quiet contemplation for 10 minutes, going to daily Mass, etc.

Some years ago, I decided I wanted to go on retreat, but I hadn't been on one since high school, almost 30 years earlier. I didn't know where to begin in terms of finding a center or style of retreat. Soon after, my parish announced it would be sponsoring a 27-hour women's retreat at a nearby retreat house. Even with my busy schedule, I knew I could afford one day away from my family. The Cornerstone retreat included talks by various members of the team, group discussions, sharing, guided prayer sessions, private prayer, a wine and cheese party, Mass, and even an opportunity to make the Communion bread, with each of us taking a turn pouring and stirring and kneading.

My Cornerstone experience opened the door to other longer and more intense retreats in the years that have followed, from my first silent retreat in a directed group setting in the Adirondack Mountains; to my entirely silent private retreat at the Abbey of the Genesee near Rochester, New York; to the Boy Scout retreat at the Auriesville shrine; to a recent yoga-prayer retreat at Kripalu Yoga Center in Lenox, Massachusetts. Each experience offered different opportunities and insights, new ways to enter into prayer, and renewed zeal for my faith. My eventual goal is to spend an entire week on silent retreat at some point in the near future.

Don't feel as though you have to jump into the deep end right off the bat. Start slowly. You may even be able to find a half-day retreat or day of recollection at a nearby parish to get your feet wet. Slowly wade deeper into the spiritual waters of silence, solitude, and contemplation so that when you eventually arrive in that stark spiritual place, you're ready for all that will unfold.

In a perfect world, you would get away on a retreat for a weekend or more at least once a year. Actually, I believe once a season would really be ideal, but most of us can't pull that off. So aim for an annual retreat. You can combine a retreat with a pilgrimage by seeking out monasteries in new places, making your journey to the retreat location part of the overall experience.

Notes from the Journey

When I headed to my first private silent retreat at the Cistercian Abbey of the Genesee near Rochester, I decided ahead of time to make the 4-hour drive part of my retreat. I took only spiritual music and one recorded talk by famed theologian Henri Nouwen. I didn't call anyone on my cell phone. I didn't talk to myself. I didn't even sing along with my favorite songs. I wanted to immerse myself in silence bit by bit, mile by mile.

By the time I was within an hour of the abbey, Henri Nouwen was talking about "A Spirituality of Waiting," and I realized that this would be a theme of my weekend, something that was confirmed the next day when I opened a random book that echoed the exact same sentiments.

Without the driving meditation to pave the way, my retreat weekend would not have begun until I arrived at Genesee, and I might have missed out on the spiritual insights gained while moving at 65 mph.

INTERIOR PILGRIMAGE

Regardless of where you go on a physical pilgrimage, or *if* you go, the reality is that you're already deeply engrossed in the most fantastic pilgrimage of all. This journey to the depths of your own heart and soul has the potential to be more satisfying and utterly transforming, if you're willing to go wherever the interior road map—drawn by the Spirit—may lead.

When you plan and then go on an actual pilgrimage, you may take comfort in the feeling of control, or at least the illusion of control at the outset. You know your destination; you've got a plan. You read guidebooks, make hotel reservations, and book airline tickets and tour packages, assuming you're the one pulling the strings. But somewhere along the way, glitches arise. A plane is delayed, a museum is closed, or a fellow traveler gets ill, and before you know it, your pilgrimage has taken off in unplanned directions to destinations unknown.

The interior journey is like that—times 10. You can sit down to prayer and think you know where you're headed. You have specific people and intentions to pray for. You say a Rosary. You listen to soothing music. From all outward appearances, even your inward journey has some element of control to it. But once you're on your way, you'll find internal delays and glitches and detours have taken you off the route you thought you were on, only to dump you into the middle of a spiritual ocean or dark wood. And that's precisely where you'll make your best and most powerful discoveries.

CULTIVATING A PILGRIM SPIRIT

If you approach your entire life with a pilgrim mind-set, you can find places that feed your heart and spirit at just about every turn—from the little shrine in the next town to the cathedral in your diocese to that historic church near your favorite vacation spot.

Start to look at the everyday moments and events of your life as pilgrim moments as well. Anything can become a pilgrimage: a journey through illness, divorce, or the death of a loved one; the 9 months of pregnancy as you prepare for the birth of a child; a new job; a marriage that has its ups and downs and twists and turns; even a new driving route to work can become a pilgrimage if you approach it as a path that can show you new ways to grow closer to Christ.

Practical Wisdom

A door opens to the center of our being and we seem to fall through it into the immense depths which, although they are infinite, are all accessible to us.

—Thomas Merton

GOING FORWARD …

- † A pilgrimage can take you out of your typical spiritual routine and breathe new life into your prayer practice.

- † While pilgrim journeys to far-off sacred sites can be especially powerful, any visit to a special holy place with the intention of deepening your connection to God is a pilgrimage.

- † Regular retreats—annually, if possible—reinvigorate your spiritual life and give you new direction for the next step on your path.

- † The ultimate pilgrimage is an interior one, a journey to the innermost recesses of your heart and soul, where you can meet God.

- † By developing a "pilgrim spirit," you can turn any moment into a spiritual journey that opens your eyes and heart to God at work in the world around you.

10

ALL OF LIFE AS PRAYER

I'm not one for pithy quotes posted on big signs outside churches. I typically find them distracting at best or silly at worst. But when I drove by the local Reform church in my town yesterday, the posted comment hit home:

> You don't change the message; the message
> changes you.

I found myself giving a little "Amen!" as I turned onto a side street. We live in a world that demands we change with the times, but faith demands just the opposite. This message—as witnessed in the person of Jesus Christ, in the stories of Gospels, in the lives of the saints and everyday Christians over the centuries—hasn't changed. It can't change, at least not if you hope to be changed by it, to be made new in Christ. His message must become your message, your way of life.

Through everyday prayer, spiritual reading, Mass, pilgrimages, retreats, and the many other practices and methods you've read about in this book, you are opening yourself daily to that message, allowing it to sink in and become part of your core.

When I think of "the message," classic lines of Scripture run through my head: God is love ... With God all things are possible ... Seek and you will find ... The Lord is my light and my salvation ... I am the way, the truth, and the life ... Love your neighbor as yourself ... I am with you always, until the end of the age ... I am the Bread of Life ... Be still and know that I am God.

What part of the message has come burning through your prayer life like rays of sun piercing the clouds on a hazy day? How has the message changed you so far? Has everyday prayer begun to shift the way you hear things, see things, or do things? Has it become a way of life?

Pope Benedict XVI, during his general audience on April 25, 2012, talked about the importance of the spiritual essentials—prayer and the word of God—in shaping daily life. Together they serve as an anchor in this ever-changing world.

"In every age the saints have stressed the deep vital unity between contemplation and activity. Prayer, nourished by faith and enlightened by God's word, enables us to see things in a new way and to respond to new situations with the wisdom and insight bestowed by the Holy Spirit," Pope Benedict said. "In our own daily lives and decisions, may we always draw fresh spiritual breath from the two lungs of prayer and the word of God; in this way, we will respond to every challenge and situation with wisdom, understanding and fidelity to God's will."

The "two lungs" of prayer and the word of God—what a powerful and life-giving image, one you can keep in mind as you continue this journey on your own in the days and years to come. Prayer is not a luxury; it is your lifeline.

Transformed from the Outside In

When it comes to transformation, you may be hoping for something momentous—a thunderclap, an "aha!" moment that will change you all at once, a sudden conversion that makes you new in every way. But sometimes—most times—transformation comes in the still, small voice, in the tiny but brilliant flashes of light that change you bit by bit, usually without your noticing it.

Instead of looking for something bold, something permanent, start watching for the subtle, seemingly insignificant changes that work their way into your life as your prayers deepen and grow—the patience you now seem to have in abundance for your children, the kindness you want to shower on a stranger in need, the calmness that descends during a crisis where before there would have been panic. The shifts don't have to be seismic to be transforming.

DOING YOUR PART, OR NOT

One night, as I lay in bed reading *Open Mind, Open Heart: The Contemplative Dimension of the Gospel* by Father Thomas Keating, I came across an observation that snapped me out of my sleepy stupor:

> Transformation is completely God's work. We can't do anything to make it happen. We can only prevent it from happening.

When I read that, my addled mind said, *Wait a minute. What was that?* I went back and read it again, knowing deep down that too often I am the one who gets in the way of my own spiritual growth, my own transformation.

Father Keating uses the Gospel story of the Canaanite woman (Matthew 15:26) as an example of how God transforms in mysterious ways. The woman comes to Jesus for healing and, as Father Keating says, gets the "cold shoulder" from the Master. He tells her, in not so many words, "Why should I waste my healing on you when my children need healing?" But she does not get angry or indignant at this turn of events. She grovels in the dust and says, "You are absolutely right, Lord. But even the dogs eat the crumbs as they fall from their master's table."

Apparently, Father Keating explains, Jesus was raising her to the "highest level of faith." In other words, sometimes to get to the glory, you have to fight your way—or more accurately, surrender your way—through what feels like rejection, confusion, abandonment, and the daily stresses of life.

"Some people complain God never answers their prayers," Father Keating writes. "Why should he? By not answering our prayers, he is answering our greatest prayer, which is to be transformed."

You may want to fixate on the end results of transformation, the glory, but if you stop and think about it, almost all transformation requires sacrifice. A caterpillar has to "die," in a sense, by shedding its former self to become a butterfly. A rainbow can appear only after a storm. You can only experience heaven by leaving this world behind.

Prayer is what gets you from here to there, whether you're talking about eternal life or meeting the demands of a fussy toddler. Everyday prayer takes your struggles and turns them into stepping stones to ultimate transformation.

Practical Wisdom

God offers holiness to us everywhere, all the time. We will receive it in great quantity from both friends and enemies. There is no better way to be "religious" than by finding God in everything that comes our way each moment.

—Jean-Pierre de Caussade, *Abandonment to Divine Providence*

HEARING THE CALL

One afternoon I had to prepare a lesson plan for my fourth-grade faith formation class based on the Gospel story of Bartimaeus, the blind man who shouts, "Jesus, Son of David, have pity on me!" (Mark 10:48) Bartimaeus kept calling out until eventually Jesus told the others to call him over. "Take courage; get up, he is calling you," they told the desperate blind man. (Mark 10:49)

To be honest, Bartimaeus had never really registered on my spiritual radar screen. When it came to Jesus giving sight to the blind, I was pretty much in the Man Born Blind camp (John 9). But trying to figure out how to explain Bartimaeus to a class of 9-year-olds forced me to dive into the Gospel in a new way. This story is meant to remind us that if we have faith and persistence, as Bartimaeus did, God will light the way for us and give us what we need to see things clearly.

My class discussion of the Gospel that day was quicker than usual because we were due in the school gym for the recitation of the Rosary. As I hurried my class down the hall—looking frazzled, I'm sure, thanks to a few rambunctious students—the Catholic school principal saw me walk by. Quite unexpectedly (I wasn't even sure I'd heard him right at first), he called out, "Take courage; get up, Jesus is calling you." And suddenly, in an instant, the story of Bartimaeus became mine in a totally new way.

For the first time, I really heard that line as it related to me. It turns out, I am very much like blind Bartimaeus, begging again and again for God to have pity on me and to help me see. My eyes are clouded by things of the external world—the busyness of life, the responsibilities of work and family, the pull of all the addictive time-drains (Twitter and Facebook and email and more)—that get too much of my attention each day.

But unlike Bartimaeus, I don't always hear God's call, drop everything, and run to Jesus. Sometimes I can't hear him over the din of everyday life. Other times, I've got my fingers in my ears because I'm afraid of what I might hear. And still other times, I'm sure my prayer life is too neglected and too erratic to warrant a response from God.

But Bartimaeus reminds us that we just have to keep praying and asking, not because we're worthy and not because we've mastered prayer, but because we believe.

God doesn't answer your prayers because you say them perfectly but because you are "shameless" in your persistence. Like Bartimaeus, you have to keep yelling out, "Jesus, have pity on me." You have to have faith and trust that he is listening and that if you make the time to listen with the "ear of your heart," you will get the answer and the sight you've been begging for, the transformation you've always imagined.

The question is, will you be ready and willing to listen to his call?

"Take courage; get up, Jesus is calling you."

One Day at a Time

If you look at your prayer life from a long-term perspective, it can intimidate you right into a state of spiritual paralysis. Even after all the spiritual work you've accomplished, you may still be wondering how you'll ever sit in silent meditation for 20 solid minutes, how you'll manage to say a Rosary every day, or how you'll ever get on a retreat every year. Before you know it, you're doing nothing.

Prayer requires a one-day-at-a-time approach, made famous by AA but transferrable to so many other parts of life. Don't start looking ahead to everything you *should* do. Just do what you can where you are right now. Remember, everyday prayer is just that—a practical, go-with-the-flow approach to spirituality that allows you to jump into prayer without a lot of external requirements.

In a *New York Times* story, "Carpe Diem? Maybe Tomorrow," writer John Tierney addresses the human propensity to procrastinate, even when something good or wonderful is at stake.

"When there is no immediate deadline, we're liable to put off going to the zoo this weekend because we assume that we will be less busy next weekend—or the weekend after that, or next summer. This is the same sort of thinking that causes us to put the gift certificate in the drawer because we expect to have more time for shopping in the future," he writes, explaining that people tend to do a "cost-benefit analysis" that convinces them to wait until they have more resources, more time, more something in the future.

"Hence you're more likely to agree to a commitment next year, like giving a speech, that you would turn down if asked to find time for it in the next month. This produces what researchers call the 'Yes ... Damn!' effect: when the speech comes due next year, you bitterly discover you're still as busy as ever," Tierney writes.

This strange but true phenomenon trickles down not only to recreational life but spiritual life as well. Despite being admonished through Scripture on a fairly regular basis to be on watch, be vigilant, and get ready because you know not the day or the hour, you may hold onto the notion that there's always tomorrow. You think to yourself, *I don't need to pray now because I'll have more time when my work project is finished or when the kids are back in school. I don't need to meditate or spend time with Scripture or get my spiritual life in order now. I'm far too busy. I'll get to it next week, next month, next year ....*

And so you wait for the ideal spiritual moment. That magical nonexistent time when the house will be quiet, the office will be neat, the incense will be burning, and the icon will be in place. But as you know, those perfect moments don't come around very often. The "perfect moment" is yours for the taking whenever you decide to stop and savor what you have right now, be it a meditative walk to get the mail or a Hail Mary said between work deadlines and the laundry.

Carpe diem. Now.

Notes from the Journey

When my youngest daughter Chiara was 4 years old, she woke up one morning and asked, "Is it tomorrow?" Just the night before she had been trying to understand the concept of yesterday, today, tomorrow. I said, "No, now it's today." She looked confused.

"It's never tomorrow," I said, finding myself just as intrigued by that notion as she was. It's never tomorrow. It's always right now. Which is a really beautiful reality, if we can learn to embrace it.

DON'T ATTEMPT TOO MUCH TOO SOON

As you embark upon or continue your prayer journey, be kind to yourself. Don't take on too much at once or expect too much too soon. This is not a race to a final destination; the journey itself is part of the payoff here. Savor it, reflect on it, and let it begin to shape who you are and where you go next.

If you set unrealistic prayer goals, there's a good chance you'll end up quitting the whole thing in frustration. Go slow. If something doesn't work for you, try something else. When life is so busy you can't imagine fitting prayer into any second of the day, fall back on short aspirations you can say even as you race from one place to another.

Always remember that everyday prayer is not meant to be a chore but a respite, an oasis of calm in a life of chaos. Don't let it become one more thing you *have* to get done. Let it be something you look forward to, something that lifts you up.

CONTINUE TO EXPLORE

Your prayer needs are likely to change year by year, day by day, sometimes even hour by hour, depending on where you are on your life journey. Try to keep your heart and mind open to different styles of prayer and different opportunities for spiritual growth. What doesn't fit you now may be perfect a year from now or 20 years from now.

Explore new styles and keep them in the back of your mind for those times when they just might be exactly what you need. Maybe you're not ready for silence just yet. That's okay. Someday you're likely to crave it. Maybe you don't like to pray with music. You don't need to, but just remember down the road, when a song opens you suddenly and you feel the Spirit rush in, that music can be your prayer. Maybe an annual retreat is impossible with your current schedule. Just file away that information until your situation changes, but do what you can to take even one afternoon for the briefest retreat.

Look back at where you were on your prayer journey 10 years ago, 10 months ago, or 10 weeks ago. Chances are, you've changed dramatically in that time. But you won't notice it until you reflect on it.

My prayer life today is far different from what it was 10 years ago. Where before I was simply happy to get something out of Sunday Mass while a fussy baby clawed at my hair, today my spiritual routine includes praying parts of the Divine Office daily, slices of silence sprinkled throughout my days, regular spiritual reading and sporadic spiritual blogging, an annual retreat, and the desire for ongoing pilgrimage—whether to Rome or a local shrine or simply to the farthest reaches of my heart.

I didn't really notice those changes as they were happening, but now they seem so clear. Just know that the same will be true of your spiritual life. Although every person is different, one thing is constant: change. Life changes, people change, prayer changes. Don't feel as though the prayer you say now must be the prayer you say always. Let your spiritual life change with you so it's always nourishing, always comforting, always relevant.

DON'T GO IT ALONE

In our fiercely independent society, there's an inclination to want to do everything on your own. But prayer requires community, at least some of the time. Don't try to make this journey a solo flight.

In Chapter 6, I talked about the need for spiritual companions. It's important to seek out spiritual friends to walk with you on your journey and maybe even a spiritual director, someone who can offer guidance, provide suggestions for your prayer life, and more than anything else, listen to your struggles and concerns.

When you first start out on a path to deeper prayer, your tendency might be to think you should seek spiritual direction or other forms of spiritual community only *after* you've achieved a certain level of holiness. Wrong. Those are precisely the things that help you move forward. If you waited until you had all the answers and had a "perfect" prayer life, you wouldn't need spiritual direction; you'd be the spiritual director.

The spiritual journey is meant to be communal. Surround yourself with others who share your hunger for deeper prayer. Seek out spiritual book clubs, prayer groups, and parish ministries that weave prayer into service activities. Take advantage of the many resources available to you through your parish, your diocese, and any religious communities that have monasteries or retreat centers in your area. There you will find a wealth of spiritual support.

Moving Meditation

If you don't already receive your local Catholic newspaper, call your parish or diocese and request a subscription. Often it's free to registered parishioners; if not, the cost is usually minimal. You'll get regular updates on upcoming spiritual events, days of recollection, retreats, and more. Plus, you'll find columns and stories to shore up your faith life.

ON THE BREATH OF GOD

St. Hildegard of Bingen, the twelfth-century German visionary, mystic, composer, and writer, once told this story:

> Listen: there was once a king sitting on his throne. Around him stood great and wonderfully beautiful columns ornamented with ivory, bearing the banners of the king with great honour. Then it pleased the king to raise a small feather from the ground, and he commanded it to fly. The feather flew, not because of anything in itself but because the air bore it along. Thus am I, a feather on the breath of God.

You, too, are called to be a "feather on the breath of God." But how? Think about the way a feather floats through the air, without resistance, without tension, without any planned destination or even direction. It goes where the wind blows. Through prayer that takes you deeper and deeper into the heart of God, you will find the courage and strength to become a delicate feather. In weakness you will become strong. In surrender you will find your destiny. That requires a willingness on your part to shed your attachment to things of this world, to relinquish control, to trust. Can you trust?

FEELING THE MOVEMENT OF THE SPIRIT

In a reflection from *Nearer to the Heart of God: Daily Readings with the Christian Mystics*, Richard Baxter, a seventeenth-century British minister, talks about how God is "in earnest" with us even when we're not in earnest with him. The Holy Spirit is "grieved" when we resist him, and God is "afflicted with us" and regards every "groan and sigh" we utter, he explains.

Grieved and *afflicted* are usually words that convey negative feelings, but in this case, those words are flipped on their head. God yearns for you, aches for your attention. What a beautiful reality.

Baxter's passage made me flash back to the days when I was writing *The Complete Idiot's Guide to the Catholic Catechism*. I was working on a chapter on the Holy Spirit and came to a quote from St. Paul, who says the Holy Spirit is the "master of prayer" who intercedes in our lives "with sighs too deep for words." (Romans 8:26–27) I remember that phrase hitting me like a ton of bricks as I was writing. I just stopped everything I was doing to soak it in.

What do you feel when you imagine the Spirit sighing on your behalf, breathing life into your life, grieving when you're unaware of its presence? As you go about your busy life, take a moment to listen for the sighs of the Spirit whispering in the background. Open a door and let the Spirit slip in. The Spirit is your guide on this journey toward God; don't leave home without it.

Do not look outside; return to yourself. In our interior the truth resides.

—St. Augustine

Resting in the Arms of God

When it comes down to it, everyday prayer is meant to bring us to a point of total surrender to God, a place where we rest on God's arms like a baby gently rocked by a doting parent.

In Psalm 139, we get a glimpse of the way God loves each one of us so completely, so tenderly, so unconditionally:

> You formed me in my inmost being;
> You knit me in my mother's womb.
> So wonderfully you made me;
> wonderful are your works!
> My very self you knew;
> my bones were not hidden from you.
> When I was being made in secret,
> fashioned as in the depths of the earth,
> Your eyes foresaw my actions;
> in your book all are written down;
> my days were shaped, before one came to be.
>
> —Psalm 139:13–16

It's no wonder we humans spend so much of our lives searching and yearning, trying to find our God, trying to know him as he knows us.

St. Augustine once said, "Our hearts are restless until they rest in you, O Lord." Your desire for deeper prayer is an outward sign of that inner restlessness. You long to rest in God, a holy rest, but how can you make that happen in a world of perpetual movement and unrest?

In his beautiful book *The Sun and Moon Over Assisi: A Personal En-counter with Francis and Clare*, author Gerard Thomas Straub takes readers along on his journey from Los Angeles to Assisi, from athe-ist to believer. He speaks of his inability to pray and feel God close to him on a daily basis. Day by day, however, as he walks the paths of Assisi and learns about the total devotion of St. Francis, his heart begins to open to a new way of thinking, a new way of being.

"Spiritual truth cannot be taught … it must be experienced," he writes. "And once it has been experienced, one instantly realizes how much there is to learn. If you want a deeper experience of God, pray for it, search for it. For every sincere step we take toward God, God takes ten toward us."

Imagine God taking 10 steps toward you every time you pray, every time you long for him. Imagine God waiting with open arms to catch you in a restfulness that cannot be disturbed or destroyed by the frenzy around you. Find your rest in God.

MAKING EVERY MOMENT A PRAYER

When I returned from a wonderful weekend retreat, the sense of peace surrounding my heart and penetrating my soul was almost palpable, unflappable. Kids did dopey things. I didn't yell. Work deadlines went from bad to worse. I didn't melt. The car bumper was bashed in by a hit-and-run meanie. I didn't explode.

In the initial days after my retreat, I kept up some semblance of deep prayer and deep peace. I cleared the decks and sat down in silent meditation in my sacred space. I did yoga followed by more prayer. I got up early and prayed the Liturgy of the Hours in the twinkling glow of the Christmas tree set against a backdrop of winter darkness.

But bit by bit, day by day, the peace started to fragment. I could almost see it happening—sharp shards of silence breaking off and flying away from me in every direction. I knew enough to realize it was an unhappy development but felt powerless to stop it.

Then I remembered something our leader said on retreat, something that really jumped out at me as I sat cross-legged on the floor. So often, when we think of Jesus in prayer, we think of him in the desert, in the garden, or in silent solitude. But the truth is that Jesus was more often than not surrounded by chaos—people clamoring to get near him, touch his robe, lower a friend through a roof, climb a tree.

"Contemplation is a loving look at the real," Paulist Father Tom Ryan told our retreat group, reminding us that Jesus did not stay hidden away in silent contemplation but took his prayer into the world, allowing it to inform and form his responses to the people he met and his day-to-day actions.

In the Gospel stories, Jesus' peace and prayerfulness emerge from amid the chaos. The quiet compassion given to the woman caught in adultery, the feeding of the 5,000, the healing of a soldier's servant, the forgiveness of a thief from the cross. Jesus did not become unloving, harsh, and impatient when the conditions around him went from good to bad to abominable. He stayed true to his center, his truth, bringing his peace into the noise and glare of an often unkind world, rather than letting it happen the other way around.

He challenges you to do the same by bringing your prayer to him in the details of daily life so he can walk with you. Jesus will help you pick up the scattered fragments of peace and fashion them into something usable, something new. Imagine this peace in daily life as a kaleidoscope of love—pieces of peace, artfully arranged into something that will cast a brilliant and warm light on everything its shooting and darting rays touch as you turn it gently in your hands.

Chaos into calm. Panic into peace. Fragments into fullness. That's what everyday prayer can bring to your life—all through him, who was ... and is ... and is to come.

Going Forward ...

† A life of everyday prayer will transform you—maybe not all at once but in small and subtle ways over time.

† Persistence, not perfection, is what counts in an everyday prayer life.

† Don't look at your spiritual life from a long-term perspective; take it day by day.

† Your prayer life will change over the years, days, and even hours. Continue to explore new styles of prayer that suit you at different times.

† Seek out a spiritual community or spiritual director who can walk this journey with you. You're not meant to go it alone.

† Everyday prayer, when lived in the light of Jesus Christ, turns every moment, even your entire life, into a continuous prayer of praise and thanksgiving.

A

FAVORITE PRAYERS

Some prayers are essential to Catholic life; others are old favorites that provide variety and inspiration as you begin to expand your everyday prayer experience. In this appendix, you'll find a collection of traditional prayers that will come in handy as you begin to weave prayer into different aspects of your daily life.

SIGN OF THE CROSS

In the name of the Father
and of the Son
and of the Holy Spirit.
Amen.

OUR FATHER (LORD'S PRAYER)

Our Father, who art in heaven,
hallowed be thy name;
thy kingdom come;
thy will be done on earth as it is in heaven.
Give us this day our daily bread,
and forgive us our trespasses,
as we forgive those who trespass against us;
and lead us not into temptation,
but deliver us from evil.
Amen.

HAIL MARY

Hail Mary, full of grace,
the Lord is with thee.
Blessed art thou among women,
and blessed is the fruit of thy womb, Jesus.
Holy Mary, Mother of God,
pray for us sinners,
now and at the hour of our death.
Amen.

GLORY BE

Glory be to the Father
and to the Son
and to the Holy Spirit,
as it was in the beginning,
is now and ever shall be,
world without end.
Amen.

APOSTLES' CREED

I believe in God,
the Father Almighty,
creator of heaven and earth,
and in Jesus Christ, his only Son, our Lord,
who was conceived by the power
of the Holy Spirit,
and born of the Virgin Mary.
He suffered under Pontius Pilate,
was crucified, died, and was buried.
He descended into hell.
On the third day he rose again.
He ascended into heaven and
and is seated at the

right hand of the Father.
He shall come again to judge
the living and the dead.
I believe in the Holy Spirit,
the holy catholic Church,
the communion of saints,
the forgiveness of sins,
the resurrection of the body,
and life everlasting.
Amen.

PRAYER TO THE HOLY SPIRIT

Come, Holy Spirit,
fill the hearts of your faithful,
and enkindle in them the fire of your love.
Send forth your Spirit and they shall be created.
And you shall renew the face of the earth.
Let us pray.
O God, who has taught the hearts
of the faithful by the light of the Holy Spirit,
grant that by the gift of the same Spirit
we may be always truly wise and
ever rejoice in his consolation.
We ask this through Christ our Lord.
Amen.

JESUS PRAYER

Lord Jesus Christ, Son of God, have mercy on me, a sinner.

ANGEL OF GOD

Angel of God,
my guardian dear,

to whom God's love
commits me here,
ever this day be at my side,
to light and guard,
to rule and guide.
Amen.

ACT OF CONTRITION

O my God, I am heartily sorry
for having offended Thee,
and I detest all of my sins
because of thy just punishments,
but most of all because they offend Thee,
my God, who art all good
and deserving all of my love.
I firmly resolve with the help of Thy grace
to sin no more and
to avoid the near occasion of sin.
Amen.

ALTERNATE ACT OF CONTRITION

O my God, I am sorry for my sins
with all my heart.
In choosing to wrong
and failing to do good,
I have sinned against you
whom I should love above all things.
I firmly intend, with your help,
to do penance,
to sin no more
and to avoid whatever leads me to sin.
Amen.

HAIL, HOLY QUEEN

Hail, Holy Queen,
Mother of Mercy,
our life, our sweetness, and our hope.
To thee do we cry,
poor banished children of Eve.
To thee do we send up our sighs,
mourning and weeping in this valley of tears.
Turn then, most gracious advocate,
thine eyes of mercy toward us,
and after this our exile
show unto us the blessed fruit of thy womb, Jesus.
O clement, O loving, O sweet Virgin Mary.
Pray for us, O holy Mother of God.
That we may be made worthy of the promises of Christ.
Amen.

MAGNIFICAT

My soul proclaims the greatness of the Lord,
my spirit rejoices in God my Savior,
for he has looked with favor on his lowly servant.
From this day all generations will call me blessed.
The Mighty One has done great things for me and holy is his name.
He has mercy on those who fear him in every generation.
He has shown might with his arm;
he has scattered the proud in their conceit.
He has cast down the mighty from their thrones,
and has lifted up the lowly.
He has filled the hungry with good things,
and the rich he has sent away empty.
He has come to the help of his servant Israel
for he has remembered his promise of mercy,
the promise he made to our fathers,
to Abraham and his children forever. (Luke 1:46–55)

MEMORARE

Remember, O most loving Virgin Mary,
that never was it known that anyone who fled to your protection,
implored your help or sought your intercession
was left unaided.
Inspired by this confidence,
I fly unto you, O virgin of virgins, my mother.
To you I come, before you I stand,
sinful and sorrowful.
O Mother of the Word Incarnate, despise not my petitions,
but in your mercy hear and answer me.

—St. Bernard

PRAYER FOR PEACE (PRAYER OF ST. FRANCIS)

Make me an instrument of your peace.
Where there is hatred, let me sow love.
Where there is injury, pardon,
where there is doubt, faith,
where there is despair, hope,
where there is darkness, light,
and where there is sadness, joy.
O Divine Master, grant that I may not
so much seek to be consoled, as to console;
to be understood, as to understand;
to be loved, as to love.
For it is in giving that we receive;
it is in pardoning that we are pardoned,
and it is in dying that we are born
to eternal life.
Amen.

GRACE BEFORE MEALS

Bless us, O Lord,
and these thy gifts
which we are about to receive
from thy bounty
through Christ Our Lord.
Amen.

PRAYING THE ROSARY

Holding the cross on your Rosary beads, make the Sign of the Cross
and recite the Apostles' Creed.

On the first separate bead, say the Our Father.

On each of the next three beads, say a Hail Mary.

On the next separate bead (or medal, depending on your Rosary
beads), announce the first mystery and say an Our Father.

On each of the next 10 beads, say a Hail Mary. End the decade with
a Glory Be.

Repeat the process—mystery, Our Father, Hail Mary, Glory Be—
for the next four decades until you go around the entire set of beads.
While saying each decade, reflect on the principal mysteries of
Christ's life and humanity's salvation.

End with the Hail Holy Queen.

MYSTERIES OF THE ROSARY

Joyful mysteries (recited Monday and Saturday):

> The Annunciation
> The Visitation
> The Birth of Our Lord
> The Presentation in the Temple
> The Finding of the Child Jesus in the Temple

Luminous mysteries (recited Thursday):

> The Baptism in the Jordan
> The Wedding at Cana
> The Proclamation of the Kingdom of God
> The Transfiguration
> The Institution of the Eucharist

Sorrowful mysteries (recited Tuesday and Friday):

> The Agony in the Garden
> The Scourging at the Pillar
> The Crowning with Thorns
> The Carrying of the Cross
> The Crucifixion

Glorious mysteries (recited Wednesday and Sunday):

> The Resurrection
> The Ascension of Our Lord
> The Descent of the Holy Spirit
> The Assumption of Our Lady into Heaven
> The Coronation of the Blessed Virgin Mary

ANGELUS

Catholics of old used to mark the main hours of the day—6 A.M., noon, and 6 P.M.—with this prayer, which is named for the Latin version of its opening line: *Angelus Domini nuntiavit Maria*, or "The angel of the Lord declared unto Mary."

When said in a group, it is a call-and-response type of prayer, punctuated by three Hail Marys. If you say it alone, just say both parts to yourself. Here's how it goes:

Leader: The angel of the Lord declared to Mary:

Response: And she conceived by the Holy Spirit.

Hail Mary ...

Leader: Behold the handmaid of the Lord.

Response: Be it done to me according to your word.

Hail Mary ...

Leader: And the Word was made flesh:

Response: And dwelt among us.

Hail Mary ...

Leader: Pray for us, O holy mother of God

Response: That we may be worthy of the promises of Christ.

Leader: Let us pray.

Response: Pour forth, we beseech you, O Lord,
your grace into our hearts, that we,
to whom the incarnation of Christ, your Son,
was made known by the message of an angel,
may be brought by his Passion and cross
to the glory of his resurrection,
through the same Christ our Lord.
Amen.

REGINA CAELI

During the Easter season, which runs from Easter Sunday through
Pentecost 50 days later, the *Angelus* is replaced with the *Regina Caeli*,
which means "queen of heaven." Here's how it goes:

O Queen of heaven, rejoice! Alleluia.
For he whom you did merit to bear, Alleluia,
has risen as he said. Alleluia.
Pray for us to God, Alleluia.
Rejoice and be glad, O Virgin Mary, Alleluia.

For the Lord has risen indeed. Alleluia.
Let us pray.
O God, who gave joy to the world through
the resurrection of your Son,
our Lord Jesus Christ,
grant that we may obtain,
through the virgin mother, Mary,
the joys of everlasting life.
Through the same Christ our Lord.
Amen.

STATIONS OF THE CROSS

Before each station, recite the following prayer:

We adore you, O Christ, and we praise you. Because by your holy cross you have redeemed the world.

First station: Jesus is condemned to death.

Second station: Jesus takes up his cross.

Third station: Jesus falls the first time.

Fourth station: Jesus is met by his mother.

Fifth station: Simon of Cyrene helps Jesus carry his cross.

Sixth station: Veronica wipes the face of Jesus.

Seventh station: Jesus falls a second time.

Eighth station: The women of Jerusalem mourn for our Lord.

Ninth station: Jesus falls for the third time.

Tenth station: Jesus is stripped of his garments.

Eleventh station: Jesus is nailed to the cross.

Twelfth station: Jesus dies on the cross.

Thirteenth station: Jesus is taken down from the cross.

Fourteenth station: Jesus is placed in the tomb.

LECTIO DIVINA, SACRED READING

Through this ancient monastic practice, you can use Scripture to enter into a deeper relationship with God in silence. In *Lectio Divina*, you don't simply read a Scripture passage; you allow the passage to speak to you.

You begin with the Sign of the Cross and a short prayer to the Holy Spirit for guidance and grace. There are four main stages:

Reading a passage (lectio): Here, you read your chosen Scripture passage slowly, taking notice of any words, phrases, or scenes that speak to or jump out at you.

Meditating on it (meditatio): At this point, you reflect on the line or word that spoke to you.

Praying or responding to God (oratio): Here, you offer a spontaneous prayer to God, expressing what you're thinking or feeling.

Contemplating or listening for God to respond (contemplatio): In this last stage, you sit in silence and "rest" in God. Just let your heart speak without words or thoughts or actions. Wait patiently for God to speak to you. This is where contemplation begins.

MEDITATION

As with *Lectio Divina*, begin your meditation in a quiet place with the Sign of the Cross and a prayer to the Holy Spirit. You can choose something specific to meditate on—the mysteries of the Rosary, the Stations of the Cross, a scene from the Gospels, or the Passion of Christ. Although at first you may simply need to sit and get used to this kind of deep silent prayer, eventually you'll want to work through these four basic steps:

† Placing yourself in the presence of God

† Asking for God's help

† Meditating on your chosen subject, image, or passage

† Giving thanks to God

LITURGY OF THE HOURS

Although every "hour" will differ day by day, here's a breakdown of a typical round of Morning or Evening Prayer in brief:

Invitatory, which is a psalm said before whichever "hour" you choose to begin the Divine Office, but not necessary if you're using a shorter form.

Introductory prayer: "God, come to my assistance. Lord, make haste to help me. Glory to the Father and to the Son and to the Holy Spirit, as it was in the beginning, is now, and will be forever. Amen." (Notice this is a slightly different version of the Glory Be than what's listed earlier in this appendix. This adapted version is typically used for the Liturgy of the Hours.)

A hymn. (You may want to skip this if you're praying alone.)

Psalms and Old and New Testament *canticles*, which are kinds of biblical songs, and *antiphons*, which are responses before and after the psalms and canticles.

Reading from Scripture.

Responsory.

One of the Gospel canticles, either the *Magnificat* (Canticle of Mary), said during Evening Prayer, or the *Benedictus* (Canticle of Zechariah), said during Morning Prayer.

Prayers of intercession.

Our Father.

Concluding prayer and verse.

When you purchase a copy of the Liturgy of the Hours, purchase the matching guide for the current year. That gives you the specific readings, page numbers, etc. You can also get an app for your smartphone, which takes away any of the potential guesswork. It can be tricky to pray the Hours on your own in the beginning, especially on feast days or during special seasons. (Check Appendix C for suggested apps and links.)

ASPIRATIONS

Jesus, I trust in you. (Divine Mercy)

Jesus, Mary, and Joseph, I love you. Save souls.

My Lord and my God.

Praised be Jesus Christ, now and forevermore.
Yes, Lord, I believe. Help my unbelief. (Mark 9:24)

B

Prayer Practices

To keep up a lifetime of everyday prayer, you'll need to borrow practices and methods from other spiritual seekers every now and then. You can find examples in the lives of the saints, the writings of contemporary Catholics, and in the everyday actions of people you know. In this appendix, I share 10 exercises to expand on what you've already started as you worked your way through this book.

A Day in the Life

For one day, write down everything you do. Everything. Showering, eating, driving to work, watching TV, trolling Facebook, cleaning up after dinner, washing your face, etc. Make special note of the times you're doing at least two things at once—checking email while talking to your kids, making a phone call while you cook dinner, and so on.

At the end of the day, review your list and see where you can streamline. What activities use valuable energy for no end benefit? Where are the most likely places to add in everyday prayer? Cross off one unnecessary item from your daily list and add in 5 minutes of silent prayer in its place.

For one week, be faithful to your silent prayer routine. At the end of the week, note in your spiritual journal whether the change affected your prayer life and your life in general.

Every time life starts to spin out of control, do this exercise and notice where and how you spend your precious time.

MINDFULLY MUNDANE

Decide on one activity you'll do with total mindfulness today. It can be a mindful meal, a mindful cleaning project, or a mindful wait at the post office—any activity can be done mindfully.

At the outset, be relentless in your mindfulness. Don't let your cell phone, email, newspaper, or novel worm its way into your practice. Focus on every aspect of your activity.

If you're eating a mindful meal, clear the space around you, light a candle if you can, pray, taste every bite, eat slowly, and clean up afterward with just as much care. Make it mindful from start to finish.

If you're being mindful in line at the post office, do so with a slight smile on your face, nodding kindly to the people around you, maybe even praying silently for whatever intentions they hold in their hearts. Don't check your watch or make a phone call or rummage through your purse for gum. Stand and move and talk with mindfulness and awareness. Make every movement a prayer.

WALKING MEDITATION

Take 10 or 15 minutes to go for a slow, meditative walk today. If it's during a workday lunch hour, walk around the block or even around your building with total attentiveness. Notice things you usually miss when you're rushing around. Every time you feel yourself speeding up, focus on your breath and your prayerful word or "theme"—Jesus, peace, abba, love.

Don't wait for the perfect sunny, warm-but-not-too-warm day. Try a meditative walk in the rain, the snow, or the cold, and notice each time how the experience varies and how it makes you feel. Where do you see God as you walk through your world with the eyes of love and mindfulness?

Contemplative Cooking

Even if you're not a gourmet cook, you still have to eat. The next time you're making a meal, whether it's something out of a fancy cookbook or a PB&J sandwich, do it in the spirit of contemplation.

Take out the ingredients, and think about where they come from, the people involved in getting them to you, and the world that provides for your needs. As you chop vegetables or stir soup or spread jelly on bread, focus on your movements, and pray as you do so, either silently listening for what God may be saying to you or actively repeating a short prayer like the Hail Mary of Jesus Prayer over and over.

Notice how this contemplative approach to cooking and preparing your food changes the experience and even the meal itself. What other areas of your life are open to contemplative action? Try this exercise there, too.

Driving at the Speed of Prayer

The next time you get into your car, do not—I repeat, do not—reach for that radio dial as soon as you turn the ignition. Start your drive with a short prayer, maybe one to your guardian angel for safety. Then proceed on your way in silence, listening to the world around you, even the honking horns and blaring radios in other cars. When someone cuts you off in traffic, pray for that person. When you miss the light and have to wait, focus your waiting time on God or on the intentions of loved ones who need your prayers.

Notice your speed, the weather, the way the road curves, and the lawns or shops along the way. Notice the face of the driver in the car facing you at the stoplight. What might be worrying that person today? Pray for him.

Begin to recognize, as you drive with total awareness, that every person on the road with you has concerns, fears, joys, and sorrows that may cause them to do things that annoy you as a fellow driver. Forgive them, and pray that God will hold them all in his hands.

You can try this one on a bus, plane, or train as well. Pray for the people cramming their luggage into the overhead compartments, taking your armrest, sneezing uncontrollably, or getting up and down to stretch their legs. Prayer can transform any travel experience, but especially a difficult one.

TAKING IT TO THE STREETS

As your prayer life deepens and grows, you're likely to find that you want to take what you're feeling inside and move it outward. This week, check your parish bulletin or local newspaper for volunteer opportunities that will allow you to help someone in need. You don't have to build a Habitat for Humanity house; you can start with something small—a food pantry that's understocked, a collection of baby goods for mothers in need, a nursing home with lonely residents, etc.

Don't think service only counts when it's overseas or in Appalachia or the inner city. Anywhere people are in need, you can reach out as a Christian and truly live out the teachings of Jesus. "For I was hungry and you gave me food ... I was naked and you clothed me, ill and you cared for me ...." (Matthew 25:35–36) None of those things require distant travel, special shots, or foreign language classes. Even bringing the neighbor's newspaper from the end of their driveway to their front door on a rainy day is service. It doesn't have to be difficult; it just has to be sincere.

Sacred Surroundings, Simplified

If you haven't already set up your personal sacred space, now's the time to do it. (Check Chapter 6 for details.) If you do have a space, chances are the area could use some decluttering.

Look at the space you've chosen. Is it starting to collect junk around the periphery—mail you haven't opened, shoes you didn't put away, books you were using but never reshelved, dust? Take some time today to simplify your space and restore its sacred center. Replace used candles, empty old incense from the holder, and wipe down the table or shelf. Study the items you've chosen for your space and decide if there's anything you'd like to add or remove.

If you've had the space set up for a while, reflect on how it's working for you. Is it in a good location? Do you find it comforting or distracting? Is there a better location? Is it too centrally located, making it a haven for any passersby who need a place to put their stuff, or themselves, perhaps right in the middle of your meditation? A cluttered, busy sacred space makes for a cluttered, busy mind.

Unplug, Unwind, and Recharge

This may be the hardest exercise in the book. For one day, turn off your cell phone. Disconnect from the web, email, social networking, instant messenger, texting, and whatever else you do via high-tech gadgets. Don't watch television or listen to the radio. Go for one full day without all the usual crutches, and see what it's like to be disconnected from the world. Instead, read a book, visit a neighbor, write a letter, meditate, say the Rosary, or do something you wouldn't normally do on a typically plugged-in day.

At some point during this downtime, take out your spiritual journal and write how it feels to be in this place. Does it make you uncomfortable? Lonely? Free? Peaceful? If you find the lack of connection has been good for your soul, consider making this a once-a-week habit. Pick a day. If you can't do once a week, try once a month. You can even let your friends know you'll be signing off so they won't wonder why you're not responding to their messages.

WHERE YOU'VE BEEN TODAY

In Catholic prayer practice, there's something known as the "Examen," which is basically a spiritual review of your day—where you met God along the way, and where you may have ignored or rebuffed him. St. Ignatius Loyola considered this prayer practice among the most important and told his fellow Jesuits that if their lives were so busy that they could do only one spiritual practice, the Examen should be that one thing. It's that important.

Although it's most common to do the Examen before bed at night, you can do it at whatever time best suits you and makes it likely you'll continue. If you do it in the morning, simply review the day before. You can even do this more than once a day, even on the hour, if you're particularly ambitious.

Basically, here's what you need to do: put yourself in God's presence, or become aware of God's presence, as you would with any prayer. Ask for the guidance of the Spirit. Begin with a prayer of gratitude, thanking God for the blessings of your day. Go through your activities and interactions of the past day, and look for the places where you felt God at work in your life and maybe those places where you shunned God and opted for something less than Christian.

Pay attention to how you're feeling. What do those feelings mean? Is God calling you to do something you don't want to do? Express sorrow and seek mercy for those times you didn't live up to your Christian ideals. Look forward to the next day with hope, asking for the grace to meet the challenges of the day with God at your side.

Mass, Sundays, and More

It seems appropriate to end this collection of exercises with the one practice that rises above every other: the Mass.

As you know, the Mass is the ultimate prayer for Catholics, an opportunity to pray together, to hear God's word, to share in the Eucharist. Mass is a critical element in any Catholic prayer life.

Sundays are, of course, the obvious time for Mass, but try to go to daily Mass if and when you can. This week, check the schedules of local churches and find one daily Mass you can attend in addition to Sunday Mass. If you don't typically go to daily Mass, notice how it's different from Sunday celebrations. Perhaps it's more intimate, in a chapel instead of a church. People may offer personal intentions during the prayer of the faithful. Although fewer people will be in attendance than at Sunday Mass, it's likely many people know each other. Daily Mass–goers tend to be pretty regular, so there's an element of familiarity that's often not present at larger Sunday celebrations, especially in big parishes.

During special seasons, daily Mass is a great addition to your usual spiritual practice. Consider adding even one daily Mass each week to your Lenten or Advent prayer practice.

C

EVERYDAY RESOURCES

As you progress on your prayer journey, it helps to have resources for more information, support, encouragement, and inspiration. Here are some ideas to get you started, but be sure to explore on your own and add to the list.

CATHOLIC BASICS

Bishops' Committee on Liturgy, National Conference of Catholic Bishops. *Catholic Household Blessings and Prayers.* Washington, DC: The Liturgical Press, 1989.

Christian Prayer: The Liturgy of the Hours. New York, NY: Catholic Book Publishing Corp., 1976.

The New American Bible (Holy Bible). Iowa Falls, IA: World Bible Publishers, Inc., 1991.

Poust, Mary DeTurris. *The Complete Idiot's Guide to the Catholic Catechism.* Indianapolis, IN: Alpha Books, 2008.

St. Benedict of Nursia. *The Rule of St. Benedict.* Garden City, NY: Image Books, 1975.

Vaticana, Libreria Editrice. *Catechism of the Catholic Church, Second Edition.* Washington, DC: USCCB Publishing, 1997.

SUGGESTED READING

Alborghetti, Marci. *A Willing Heart: How to Serve When You Think You Can't*. Notre Dame, IN: Ave Maria Press, 2011.

Bangley, Bernard, ed. *Nearer to the Heart of God: Daily Readings with the Christian Mystics*. Brewster, MA: Paraclete Press, 2005.

Brother Lawrence. *The Practice of the Presence of God*. Grand Rapids, MI: Revell, 1967.

Buder, Sister Madonna, with Karin Evans. *The Grace to Race, The Wisdom and Inspiration of the 80-Year-Old World Triathlete Known as the Iron Nun*. New York, NY: Simon & Schuster, 2010.

Ciszek, Father Walter J., SJ. *He Leadeth Me*. San Francisco, CA: Ignatius Press, by arrangement with Doubleday, 1973.

d'Avila-Latourrette, Brother Victor-Antoine. *This Is Good Food: French Vegetarian Recipes from a Monastery Kitchen*. New York, NY: W.W. Norton & Co., 2012.

Dillard, Annie. *Pilgrim at Tinker Creek*. New York, NY: Quality Paperback Book Club, 1974.

Edmisten, Karen. *The Rosary: Keeping Company with Jesus and Mary*. Cincinnati, OH: Servant Books, 2009.

Ellsberg, Robert, ed. *Dorothy Day: Selected Writings*. Maryknoll, NY: Orbis Books, 1992.

Hanh, Thich Nhat. *Peace Is Every Step*. New York, NY: Bantam, 1991.

Huston, Paula. *The Holy Way: Practices for a Simple Life*. Chicago, IL: Loyola Press, 2003.

John Paul II, edited and compiled by Tony Castle. *The Way of Prayer*. New York, NY: Crossroad Publishing, 1995.

Keating, Thomas. *Open Mind, Open Heart: The Contemplative Dimension of the Gospel*. New York, NY: Continuum Publishing, 1992.

Kolodiejchuk, Brian, MC, ed. *Mother Teresa: Come Be My Light: The Private Writings of the Saint of Calcutta*. New York, NY: Doubleday, 2007.

LeClaire, Anne D. *Listening Below the Noise: A Meditation on the Practice of Silence.* New York, NY: Harper, 2009.

Markova, Dawna. *I Will Not Die an Unlived Life: Reclaiming Purpose and Passion.* Berkeley, CA: Conari Press, 2000.

Martin, James, SJ. *My Life with the Saints.* Chicago, IL: Loyola Press, 2006.

McKenna, Megan. *Praying the Rosary.* New York, NY: Doubleday, 2004.

Merton, Thomas. *New Seeds of Contemplation.* New York, NY: New Directions, 1961.

———. *Thoughts in Solitude.* New York, NY: Farrar, Straus, Giroux, 1958.

Murphy, Charles M. *The Spirituality of Fasting: Rediscovering a Christian Practice.* Notre Dame, IN: Ave Maria Press, 2010.

Norris, Kathleen. *The Cloister Walk.* New York, NY: Riverhead Books, 1996.

Nouwen, Henri J. M. *Life of the Beloved: Spiritual Living in a Secular World.* New York, NY: Crossroad Publishing, 1992.

———. *The Only Necessary Thing: Living a Prayerful Life.* New York, NY: Crossroad Publishing, 1999.

Pierce, Gregory F. *Spirituality at Work: 10 Ways to Balance Your Life on the Job.* Chicago, IL: Loyola Press, 2005.

Poust, Mary DeTurris. *The Complete Idiot's Guide to the Catholic Catechism.* Indianapolis, IN: Alpha Books, 2008.

———. *Cravings: A Catholic Wrestles with Food, Self-Image, and God.* Notre Dame, IN: Ave Marie Press, 2012.

———. *The Essential Guide to Catholic Prayer and the Mass.* Indianapolis, IN: Alpha Books, 2011.

———. *Walking Together: Discovering the Catholic Tradition of Spiritual Friendship.* Notre Dame, IN: Ave Maria Press, 2010.

Ryan, Thomas. *Reclaiming the Body in Christian Spirituality.* New York, NY/Mahwah, NJ: Paulist Press, 2004.

St. Francis de Sales. *Introduction to the Devout Life*. New York, NY: Vintage Books, 2002.

St. James, Elaine. *Simplify Your Life: 100 Ways to Slow Down and Enjoy the Things That Really Matter*. New York, NY: Hyperion, 1994.

St. Thérèse of Lisieux. *The Story of a Soul*. New York, NY: Image Books/Doubleday, 2001.

Scaperlanda, Maria Ruiz, and Michael Scaperlanda. *The Journey: A Guide for the Modern Pilgrim*. Chicago, IL: Loyola Press, 2004.

Silf, Margaret. *Wayfaring: A Gospel Journey in Everyday Life*. Notre Dame, IN: Sorin Books, 2009.

Straub, Gerard Thomas. *The Sun and Moon Over Assisi: A Personal Encounter with Francis and Clare*. Cincinnati, OH: St. Anthony Messenger Press, 2000.

Talbot, John Michael, with Steve Rabey. *The Lessons of St. Francis: How to Bring Simplicity and Spirituality into Your Daily Life*. New York, NY: Plume Publishing, 1997.

Taylor, Brian C. *Spirituality for Everyday Living: An Adaptation of the Rule of St. Benedict*. Collegeville, MN: The Liturgical Press, 1989.

Vest, Norvene. *No Moment Too Small: Rhythms of Silence, Prayer, and Holy*. Kalamazoo, MI: Cistercian Publications, 1994.

ONLINE RESOURCES

The internet provides access to an almost endless number of spiritual resources of every kind, from basic, factual websites, to inspiring blogs, to prayer pages. The following list includes the websites and blogs of those interviewed in the pages of this book, as well as other general sites.

EVERYDAY PRAYER WEBSITES:

The Catholic Foodie
catholicfoodie.com

Christians Practicing Yoga
christianspracticingyoga.com

The Goodness of the Garden
goodnessofthegarden.blogspot.com

Mary's Gardens
campus.udayton.edu/mary/resources/m_garden/marygardensmain

Not Strictly Spiritual
notstrictlyspiritual.com

Prayer Shawl Ministry
shawlministry.com

The Rosary Workout
rosaryworkout.com

OTHER HELPFUL WEBSITES:

BibleGateway.com
biblegateway.com

Bible Search Engines
usccb.org/bible

Daily Scripture Readings
usccb.org/bible/readings/052212.cfm

Liturgy of the Hours
Both of the following sites provide daily readings and prayers for the Liturgy of the Hours:

eBreviary
ebreviary.com

Universalis
universalis.com

Mass Times
masstimes.org

Sacred Space
sacredspace.ie

Word of God Everyday
wordofgodeveryday.com

Prayer Apps for Download

The following applications are among the most popular for using a handheld device to further spiritual life and prayer:

Liturgy of the Hours
Universalis
iPhone/iPad application
Universalis Publishing

Missal
iMissal
iPhone application
Cantcha, Inc.

Rosary
Rosary Miracle Prayer
iPhone/iPod application
Pauline Books and Media

INDEX

decluttering your life,
117-121
less is more concept,
118-119
ridding self of extras,
119-121
devotions (private devotions)
novenas, 26-27
Rosary, 24-26
saints and angels, 27-28
distant holy land
pilgrimages, 151-152
distractions, overcoming,
123-124

E

emptiness challenges (prayer)
accepting unanswered
prayers, 137-138
becoming a "fool for
Christ," 143-146
overview, 131-137
perseverance, 140-143
trust and surrender
concept, 139-140
essentials of prayer, 18-24
adoration, 20
blessings, 20-21
community, 22-23
Eucharist, 22
intercessions, 19
Mass, 21
petitions, 18
praise, 19-20
thanksgiving, 19

Eucharist (prayer essentials),
22
everyday prayer, 173-174
example beginner prayers,
12-13
exercises (body-spirit
connection), 51-65
dance and yoga, 59-60
hiking and camping, 57-58
illness challenges, 61-65
meditative walks, 55-57

F

fasting, 73-76
"feather on the breath of
God," 170
"fool for Christ," 143-146

G

gardening, prayerful artistic
expression, 76-78
God
nature connection, 95-102
creatures, 100-102
landscape appreciation,
96-98
storms, 98-100
surrendering to, 172-173

Q–R

S